otchbiscuits
erblueberry
mealcoffee
eadwaffles
onutcheese
cherryscone

the muffin book

Published by Fog City Press
814 Montgomery Street
San Francisco, CA 94133 USA

Copyright © 2002 Weldon Owen Pty Ltd

Chief Executive Officer: John Owen
President: Terry Newell
Publisher: Lynn Humphries
Managing Editor: Janine Flew
Art Director: Kylie Mulquin
Editorial Coordinator: Tracey Gibson
Production Manager: Martha Malic-Chavez
Business Manager: Emily Jahn
Vice President International Sales: Stuart Laurence

Project Editor: Janine Flew
Project Designer: Jacqueline Richards
Food Photography: Valerie Martin
Food Stylist: Sally Parker
Home Economist: Christine Shepherd
Recipe Development: Michelle Earl

ISBN 1 876778 83 0

Color reproduction by SC (Sang Choy) International Pte Ltd
Manufactured by Kyodo Printing Co. (S'pore) Pte Ltd
Printed in Singapore

A Weldon Owen Production

the muffin book

FOG CITY PRESS

contents

muffin magic

With the abundance of fast foods and convenience foods in our lives today, some people find themselves intimidated by the thought of cooking at home. Baking often seems particularly daunting, yet there is no need for it to be. No baked goods are easier to make, or give more reliable results, than muffins and other quickbreads such as waffles, biscuits, scones, pancakes, and tea breads.

Athough called quick "breads," these are simple mixtures that do not contain yeast, and therefore need no special treatment and no lengthy rising time. Nor do they require any exotic ingredients, advanced techniques, or specialized equipment. The batters are quickly mixed, then briefly baked. The process is simplicity itself, and it can take as little as 30 minutes to produce a batch of fragrant muffins or golden pikelets, yet the results are tender and flavorsome. Once you've mastered the art of baking muffins and quickbreads at home, you'll realize how superior they are to the commercial varieties. And because you are making each loaf or muffin from scratch, you know with total confidence that the final product is fresh, wholesome, and incomparably full of flavor.

The Muffin Book comprises two parts. Part One deals with the basics of muffin making—how to prepare ingredients and pans, mix batters, and bake to perfection—and also presents more than 90 recipes for both sweet and savory muffins. There are old favorites such as Blueberry

Muffins and Triple Chocolate Muffins, as well as modern interpretations such as Marmalade Poppyseed Muffins, Sun-dried Tomato and Camembert Muffins, and Caramelized Onion and Thyme Muffins. There are also recipes designed for the microwave oven, and others that can be prepared up to several days ahead and baked in batches as needed. As well, specially formulated recipes containing soy milk and low-fat ingredients cater for those on special diets. And, in the unlikely event that your muffins don't turn out as you'd expected, there are handy troubleshooting tips that will soon help you fix the problem.

Part Two provides information on assembling and baking quickbreads, describes the various types of quickbreads, and offers more than 55 recipes from all over the world. There are sweet treats such as Strawberry Shortcakes, Ginger Scones, and Irish Teacake, as well as savory recipes such as Rye and Raisin Bread, Beer Breads with Parmesan and Rosemary, Ratatouille Mini Pizzas, and Pumpkin and Pecan Cob.

Interspersed throughout the text are handy hints, from advice on selecting, using, and storing ingredients to ideas for recipe variations, as well as tips on techniques and equipment. Whether you're looking for savory muffins for a healthful snack, a wholesome loaf to accompany a family meal, or a sweet quickbread that will make a delicious dessert, *The Muffin Book* will provide inspiration for novice and experienced bakers alike.

part
One

muffins

muffin-making basics

Like all quick breads, muffins can be assembled in minutes and baked in a few minutes more. Because of their size, they are the easiest and fastest of any bread to prepare. Muffins require about half the baking time of a quickbread loaf because they are so much smaller. A standard muffin is 2½ inches (6 cm) in diameter and has a ½-cup (4-fl oz) capacity; a large muffin is 3 inches (8 cm), with a 1-cup (8-fl oz) capacity; and a mini muffin is 1¾ inches (4.5 cm) with a ¼-cup (2-fl oz) capacity.

Even though a recipe will specify the size of the muffin pans, you can change the size of the pans if you adjust the baking time. A recipe for 12 standard muffins will make about 6 large muffins and about 24 mini muffins. In general, bake standard muffins for 15 minutes, large muffins for about 20 minutes, and mini muffins for about 12 minutes. Use heavyweight muffin pans that absorb and hold heat so that your muffins will rise high and have a good color. Always test the muffins with a wooden toothpick or fine wooden skewer a few minutes before the end of the stated cooking time. If the toothpick or skewer comes out clean, with no batter or crumbs sticking to it, the muffins are cooked.

Muffin preparation can be done in stages if time is short. To put a batch of just-baked muffins on the breakfast table, mix the dry and liquid ingredients the night before and store them separately. The next morning, combine as directed in the recipe and bake. Alternatively, prepare a make-ahead batter such as for Fruit and Honey Bran Muffins on pages 14–15 or Refrigerator Apple Muffins on pages 20–21, or freeze the mixture as described on page 47.

steps in preparing muffins

greasing pans Using a soft pastry brush or a paper towel, spread a thin layer of butter, vegetable oil, or vegetable shortening on the bottom and three-fourths of the way up the sides of each mold. (This gives the muffins a nicely rounded top.) Keep the coating even and almost translucent so the muffins finish crisp and brown, not gummy.

lining pans Parchment (baking) paper cases are an alternative to greasing. Press 1 case into each muffin cup (be sure that the paper liner is the correct size for the cup you are using). Don't worry if the empty case doesn't sit all the way down; the batter will anchor it after it is filled.

stirring until moistened Make a well in the center of the combined dry ingredients and add the combined liquid ingredients. With a fork or wooden spoon, stir together until the flour mixture is just moistened (it will still be lumpy). Don't overstir, or the muffins will be tough.

adding extra ingredients Drop berries, nuts, or other additions on top of the batter. Gently fold them in with a rubber spatula, using a down, up, and over motion. Be careful not to crush berries or over-handle the batter. The berries will be thoroughly incorporated, but the batter will still show lumps and traces of flour.

filling prepared pans Scoop up batter with a spoon. Use a teaspoon for mini muffins and a tablespoon for standard or large muffins. Use another spoon to push the batter off into the prepared muffin cups. Fill them two-thirds full; less batter will produce small muffins, while more will overflow onto the flat surface of the pan.

removing muffins from pan After baking, loosen muffins by running a small metal spatula or knife around their sides, between the muffin and the pan. (Paper-wrapped muffins don't need to be loosened.) Muffins are best eaten warm. If not serving immediately, transfer them from the pan to a wire rack and allow to cool.

sweet *muffins*

basic muffins

makes 10 plain or
12 fruit standard muffins

1¾ cups (9 oz/280 g)
all-purpose (plain) flour

2 teaspoons baking powder

¼ teaspoon salt

⅓ cup (3 oz/90 g) sugar

1 egg, beaten

¾ cup (6 fl oz/185 ml) milk

¼ cup (2 fl oz/60 ml)
vegetable oil

¾ cup (3 oz/90 g) fresh or
frozen blueberries, pitted
cherries, or peeled, diced
peaches or apples (optional)

1 teaspoon finely shredded
lemon zest (optional)

❖ Preheat oven to 400°F (200°C/Gas Mark 5). Grease ten or twelve standard (½-cup) muffin cups or line them with parchment (baking) paper cases.

❖ In a medium mixing bowl, sift together the flour, baking powder, and salt. Stir through the sugar and make a well in the center.

❖ In a small mixing bowl, combine the egg, milk, and oil. Add all at once to the flour mixture and stir until just moistened (the batter should be lumpy). Stir in the fruit and/or lemon zest, if using.

❖ Spoon batter into prepared muffin cups, filling them two-thirds full. Bake until golden brown and a wooden skewer or toothpick inserted into the center of a muffin comes out clean, about 15 minutes. Remove from oven and cool in pan for 5 minutes. Serve warm, or transfer to a wire rack to cool.

fruit and honey bran muffins

makes 16 standard muffins

This batter may be baked immediately or kept in the refrigerator for up to 3 days. Follow the directions for storing and stirring the batter given on pages 20–21 for Refrigerator Apple Muffins. These muffins taste equally good with any dried fruit, including apricots, cherries, cranberries, or dates.

1½ cups (7½ oz/235 g) all-purpose (plain) flour

1 tablespoon baking powder

1 teaspoon ground cinnamon

¼ teaspoon salt

1 cup (2½ oz/75 g) whole-bran cereal or ½ cup (2 oz/60 g) toasted wheat bran

¼ cup (2 oz/60 g) firmly packed brown sugar

1 egg, lightly beaten

1¼ cups (10 fl oz/315 ml) milk

¼ cup (3 fl oz/90 ml) honey

¼ cup (2 fl oz/60 ml) vegetable oil

½ cup (2 oz/60 g) raisins or dried cranberries or (3 oz/90 g) chopped dried fruit (apricots, dates, or cherries)

Preheat oven to 400°F (200°C/Gas Mark 5). Grease sixteen standard (½-cup) muffin cups or line them with parchment (baking) paper cases.

In a medium mixing bowl, sift together the flour, baking powder, cinnamon, and salt. Stir through the whole-bran cereal or toasted wheat bran and brown sugar. Make a well in the center.

In a small mixing bowl, combine the egg, milk, honey, and oil. Add all at once to the flour mixture and stir until just moistened (the batter should be lumpy). Fold in the fruit.

Spoon batter into prepared muffin cups, filling them two-thirds full. Bake until golden brown and a wooden skewer or toothpick inserted into the center of a muffin comes out clean, 15–20 minutes. Remove from oven and cool in pan for 5 minutes. Serve warm, or transfer to a wire rack to cool.

troubleshooting tips

If your muffins disappoint, check the possible reason.

muffins brown on top before cooking through Oven was too hot; pan was placed too near top of oven.

muffins don't rise enough Batter was allowed to sit too long before baking; oven heat was too low.

muffins have uneven tops Oven heat was too high.

muffins have hard, shiny tops and interior tunnels Batter was overmixed.

muffins stick to the pan Pan was not greased sufficiently, or muffins were left sitting too long in pan after its removal from oven.

muffin tops spread too much Too much batter was put into each cup.

raspberry–cream cheese muffins

makes 18 standard muffins

These muffins will be the first things to disappear from your brunch table! Fresh or frozen raspberries add a sweet tang that blends flawlessly with the rich cream-cheese flavor.

2 cups (10 oz/315 g) all-purpose (plain) flour

2 teaspoons baking powder

3/4 teaspoon ground cinnamon

1/4 teaspoon baking soda (bicarbonate of soda)

1/4 teaspoon salt

1/2 cup (3 1/2 oz/105 g) packed brown sugar

1/2 cup (4 oz/125 g) cream cheese (plain or with strawberries)

2 eggs, beaten

3/4 cup (6 fl oz/185 ml) milk

1/4 cup (2 oz/60 g) butter, melted

1/2 teaspoon vanilla extract (essence)

1 cup (4 oz/125 g) fresh or frozen raspberries

confectioners' (icing) sugar (optional)

✧ Preheat oven to 400°F (200°C/Gas Mark 5). Grease eighteen standard (½-cup) muffin cups or line them with parchment (baking) paper cases.

✧ In a medium mixing bowl, stir together the flour, baking powder, cinnamon, baking soda, and salt. Stir through the brown sugar. Using a pastry blender, cut in the cream cheese until the mixture resembles crumbs about the size of a pea.

✧ In a small mixing bowl, combine eggs, milk, melted butter, and vanilla extract. Add all at once to the flour mixture and stir until just moistened (the batter should be lumpy).

✧ Fold in the raspberries. Spoon batter into prepared muffin cups, filling them two-thirds full. Bake until golden brown and a wooden skewer or toothpick inserted into the center of one of the muffins comes out clean, about 15 minutes. Remove from oven and cool in pan for 5 minutes. Serve warm, or transfer to a wire rack to cool.

✧ If desired, sift a little confectioners' sugar over the tops of the muffins before serving.

sour cherry muffins
with crumb topping

makes 6 large or
12 standard muffins

Use the same fruit you'd
put into a pie for these
muffins: tart red cherries
that hold up well in baking,
such as Montmorency.
Sweeter Bings can be used
too, although they soften
up much more. Chop the
cherries coarsely to get
some in every bite.

CRUMB TOPPING

¼ cup (2 oz/60 g) packed brown sugar

2 tablespoons all-purpose (plain) flour

2 tablespoons butter

MUFFINS

1¾ cups (9 oz/280 g) all-purpose (plain) flour

2 teaspoons baking powder

¼ teaspoon salt

¼ teaspoon ground nutmeg

⅓ cup (3 oz/90 g) granulated (white) sugar

1 egg, beaten

¾ cup (6 fl oz/185 ml) milk

¼ cup (2 fl oz/60 ml) vegetable oil

1 cup (5 oz/155 g) pitted tart red cherries (fresh,
frozen, or drained canned), coarsely chopped

❖ Preheat oven to 400°F (200°C/Gas Mark 5). Grease six large (1-cup) or twelve standard (½-cup) muffin cups or line them with parchment (baking) paper cases.

❖ For crumb topping, in a small mixing bowl, combine the brown sugar and flour. With a pastry blender, two knives, or your fingertips, cut in the butter until the mixture resembles coarse crumbs; set aside.

❖ For muffins, in a large mixing bowl, sift together the flour, baking powder, salt, and nutmeg. Stir through the granulated sugar. Make a well in the center.

❖ In a medium mixing bowl, combine the egg, milk, and oil. Add all at once to the flour mixture and stir until just moistened (the batter should be lumpy). Stir in the cherries.

❖ Spoon batter into prepared muffin cups, filling them two-thirds full. Sprinkle topping over muffins. Bake until golden brown and a wooden skewer or toothpick inserted into the center of a muffin comes out clean, about 25 minutes for large muffins or 20 minutes for standard muffins. Remove from oven and cool in pan for 5 minutes. Serve warm, or transfer to a wire rack to cool.

refrigerator apple muffins

makes 18 standard muffins

The egg whites and skim milk in this recipe help reduce the amount of fat. You can make this batter ahead of time and store it in the refrigerator for up to 3 days.

To make your own apple pie spice, combine 2 teaspoons ground cinnamon, 1 teaspoon ground nutmeg, ½ teaspoon ground allspice, and ½ teaspoon ground ginger.

¾ cup (4 oz/125 g) all-purpose (plain) flour

1 tablespoon baking powder

1 tablespoon apple pie spice (see note)

½ teaspoon baking soda (bicarbonate of soda)

½ teaspoon salt

1½ cups (9 oz/280 g) quick-cooking multi-grain cereal or muesli

1 cup (7 oz/220 g) firmly packed brown sugar

1 cup (5 oz/155 g) whole wheat (wholemeal) flour

⅓ cup (1 oz/30 g) toasted wheat germ

1½ cups (6 oz/185 g) chopped peeled cooking apples (such as Jonathan, Granny Smith, or Bramley)

3 egg whites or 2 eggs, lightly beaten

1¼ cups (6 fl oz/185 ml) skim milk

⅓ cup (3 fl oz/90 ml) vegetable oil

coarse sugar or granulated sugar

✣ In a large mixing bowl, sift together the all-purpose flour, baking powder, apple pie spice, baking soda, and salt. Stir through the cereal or muesli, brown sugar, whole wheat flour, and wheat germ. Add the apples; stir well.

✣ In a small mixing bowl, combine the egg whites or eggs, milk, and oil. Add all at once to the flour mixture and stir until just moistened (the mixture should be lumpy).

✣ Place the muffin batter in an airtight container. Cover, seal, and label with the date by which it must be used. Store in the refrigerator for up to 3 days.

✣ When ready to bake, preheat oven to 400°F (200°C/Gas Mark 5). Grease eighteen standard (½-cup) muffin cups or line them with parchment (baking) paper cases. Gently stir the batter (it will have risen during storage), then spoon into prepared muffin cups, filling them two-thirds full. Sprinkle each muffin top with some of the coarse or granulated sugar.

✣ Bake until golden brown and a wooden skewer or toothpick inserted into the center of a muffin comes out clean, 15–18 minutes. Remove from oven and cool in pan for 5 minutes. Serve warm, or transfer to a wire rack to cool.

orange blossom
mini muffins

makes 24 mini
or 12 standard muffins

These light and airy muffins
are adorned with shredded
orange zest and a dusting of
sugar. To shred zest, using a
vegetable peeler, pare away
long, 1-inch (2.5-cm) wide
strips of the colored peel
from an orange. Avoid the
bitter white pith beneath.
With a small paring knife,
cut each strip into very
thin matchsticks.

2 teaspoons sugar

3 teaspoons finely shredded orange zest

1½ cups (7½ oz/235 g) all-purpose (plain) flour

1½ teaspoons baking powder

⅛ teaspoon salt

½ cup (4 oz/125 g) sugar

1 egg, beaten

½ cup (4 fl oz/125 ml) milk

¼ cup (2 oz/60 g) butter, melted

2 tablespoons frozen orange juice concentrate, thawed

❖ Preheat oven to 400°F (200°C/Gas Mark 5). Lightly grease twenty-four mini (¼-cup) or twelve standard (½-cup) muffin cups or line them with parchment (baking) paper cases.

❖ For topping, in a small bowl, combine the 2 teaspoons sugar and 1 teaspoon of the shredded orange zest, pressing zest into sugar with the back of a spoon; set aside.

❖ For muffins, in a large mixing bowl, stir together the flour, baking powder, salt, and the remaining 2 teaspoons finely shredded orange zest. Stir through the ½-cup (4 oz/125 g) sugar. Make a well in the center.

❖ In a small mixing bowl, combine the egg, milk, melted butter, and orange juice concentrate. Add all at once to the flour mixture and stir until just moistened (the batter should be lumpy).

❖ Spoon batter into prepared muffin cups, filling them two-thirds full. Sprinkle tops of muffins with sugar–orange peel mixture. Bake until golden brown and a wooden skewer or toothpick inserted into the center of a muffin comes out clean, about 12 minutes for mini muffins or 15 minutes for standard muffins. Remove from oven and cool in pan for 5 minutes. Serve warm, or transfer to a wire rack to cool.

almond-poppy seed muffins

makes 24 mini or
12 standard muffins

Make these almond-scented
muffins bite-size for a buffet
or if they are to be served
with a number of other
foods. For breakfast or
snacks, bake a batch of
larger ones.

1³/₄ cups (9 oz/280 g) all-purpose (plain) flour

2 tablespoons poppy seeds

2 teaspoons baking powder

¹/₄ teaspoon salt

¹/₂ cup (4 oz/125 g) sugar, plus 2 tablespoons extra

1 egg, beaten

³/₄ cup (6 fl oz/185 ml) milk

¹/₄ cup (2 fl oz/60 ml) vegetable oil

¹/₂ teaspoon almond extract (essence)

2 tablespoons butter, melted

❖ Preheat oven to 400°F (200°C/Gas Mark 5). Lightly grease twenty-four mini (¼-cup) or twelve standard (½-cup) muffin cups or line them with parchment (baking) paper cases.

❖ In a medium mixing bowl, sift together the flour, poppy seeds, baking powder, and salt. Stir through the ½ cup (4 oz/125 g) sugar. Make a well in the center.

❖ In a small mixing bowl, combine egg, milk, oil, and almond extract. Add all at once to the flour mixture and stir until just moistened (the batter should be lumpy).

❖ Spoon batter into prepared muffin cups, filling them two-thirds full. Bake until golden brown and a wooden skewer or toothpick inserted into the center of a muffin comes out clean, about 12 minutes for mini muffins or 15 minutes for standard muffins.

❖ Remove from oven and cool in pan for 5 minutes, then remove from pan. Dip tops into melted butter, then into the extra 2 tablespoons sugar to coat. Cool slightly on wire racks before serving.

recipe steps

dipping tops Melt the butter and pour it into a small dish. Place next to a dish of sugar. To coat the top of the muffins, grasp a muffin by its base and dip in butter. Then, dip in sugar, rolling to apply an even, all-over layer (not all the butter and sugar will be used). Let dipped muffins sit on a wire rack until needed.

cinnamon-streusel cider muffins

makes 12 standard muffins

A thick sprinkling of streusel tops a pan of these quick and easy muffins. Their mild apple flavoring is sure to please all—especially when they're served fresh from the oven.

STREUSEL TOPPING

⅓ cup (2½ oz/75 g) firmly packed brown sugar

3 tablespoons all-purpose (plain) flour

2 teaspoons ground cinnamon

3 tablespoons cold butter

MUFFINS

1¾ cups (9 oz/280 g) all-purpose (plain) flour

2 teaspoons baking powder

¼ teaspoon salt

⅓ cup (3 oz/90 g) granulated sugar

1 egg, beaten

¾ cup (6 fl oz/185 ml) apple cider or apple juice

¼ cup (2 fl oz/60 ml) vegetable oil

❖ Preheat oven to 400°F (200°C/Gas Mark 5). Grease twelve standard (½-cup) muffin cups or line them with parchment (baking) paper cases.

❖ For streusel, in a small mixing bowl, stir together the brown sugar, flour, and cinnamon. Using a pastry blender, two knives, or your fingertips, cut in the butter until the mixture resembles coarse crumbs. Set aside.

❖ For muffins, in a medium mixing bowl, sift together the flour, baking powder, and salt. Stir in the granulated sugar. Make a well in the center.

❖ In a small mixing bowl, combine the egg, cider or juice, and oil. Add all at once to the flour mixture and stir until just moistened (the batter should be lumpy).

❖ Spoon about 1 tablespoon of batter into each prepared muffin cup; sprinkle with 1 teaspoon of the brown sugar mixture. Fill two-thirds full with remaining batter. Sprinkle the tops of the muffins with the remaining topping, covering the batter evenly for the most attractive result.

❖ Bake until golden brown and a wooden skewer or toothpick inserted into the center of a muffin comes out clean, about 15 minutes. Remove from oven and cool in pan for 5 minutes. Serve warm, or transfer to a wire rack to cool.

blueberry bran muffins

makes 12 standard muffins

Blueberries are the classic muffin ingredient. These blueberry muffins have the added goodness of bran. Fresh or frozen berries may be used; if using frozen, do not thaw them before adding them to the batter, or the juice will turn the muffins grayish.

1 cup (4 oz/125 g) processed bran

1 cup (8 fl oz/250 ml) skim milk

1/2 cup (4 oz/125 g) butter, at room temperature

1 cup (6 oz/185 g) lightly packed brown sugar

1 egg

2 cups (10 oz/315 g) whole wheat (wholemeal) self-rising flour

1 teaspoon baking powder

1 cup (5 oz/155 g) fresh or frozen blueberries

✥ Preheat oven to 400°F (200°C/Gas Mark 5). Grease twelve standard (½-cup) muffin cups or line them with parchment (baking) paper cases.

✥ Soak the bran in the milk until all of the liquid is absorbed, about 30 minutes.

✥ Cream the butter and sugar until light and fluffy. Beat in the egg. Add the bran mixture. Sift together the flour and baking powder, then fold into the butter-and-sugar mixture. Mix well. Stir in the blueberries.

✥ Spoon batter into prepared muffin cups, filling them two-thirds full. Bake until golden brown and a wooden skewer or toothpick inserted into the center of a muffin comes out clean, 15–20 minutes. Remove from oven and cool in pan for 5 minutes. Serve warm, or transfer to a wire rack to cool.

recipe variations

Any kind of berry could be used in this recipe. Try finely sliced strawberries, wiped on paper towels to blot up excess juice, fresh or frozen raspberries, or a mixture of your favorite seasonal berries. For spiced muffins, add 1 teaspoon cinnamon or mixed spice to the flour before sifting it.

streusel coffee muffins

makes 6 large muffins

STREUSEL

½ cup (3½ oz/105 g) firmly packed light or dark brown sugar

½ cup (2½ oz/75 g) all-purpose (plain) flour

½ cup (2 oz/60 g) finely chopped walnuts

¼ cup (2 oz/60 g) chilled butter, cubed

MUFFINS

2 cups (10 oz/315 g) all-purpose (plain) flour

1½ teaspoons ground cinnamon

½ teaspoon ground nutmeg

1 teaspoon baking powder

1 teaspoon baking soda (bicarbonate of soda)

½ teaspoon salt

½ cup (4 oz/125 g) butter, at room temperature

¾ cup (6 oz/185 g) firmly packed dark brown sugar

2 eggs

1 cup (8 fl oz/250 ml) buttermilk, mixed with 1 teaspoon vanilla extract (essence)

1 firm yet ripe pear, such as Bosc, Anjou, or Comice, peeled, cored, and coarsely chopped

◈ Preheat oven to 375°F (190°C/Gas Mark 4). Grease six large (1-cup) muffin cups.

◈ For streusel, in a small bowl, combine the brown sugar, flour, walnuts, and butter. Using two knives, your fingertips, or a pastry blender, work the ingredients together until the mixture resembles coarse crumbs. Cover and refrigerate until ready to use.

◈ For muffins, in a large bowl, sift together the flour, cinnamon, nutmeg, baking powder, baking soda, and salt.

◈ In another large bowl, using an electric mixer set on high speed, beat the butter until light and fluffy. Gradually add the brown sugar, continuing to beat until pale, about 3 minutes. Add the eggs, one at a time, beating well after each addition.

◈ Reduce the mixer to low speed and gradually beat in the flour mixture alternately with the buttermilk, beating until just mixed.

◈ Spoon batter into prepared muffin cups, filling them two-thirds full. Scatter the chopped pear and the streusel mixture evenly over the top, then press gently into the top of the batter.

◈ Bake until tops of muffins are firm, the streusel is crisp and bubbling, and a wooden skewer or toothpick inserted into the center of a muffin comes out clean, 25–30 minutes. Remove from oven and cool in pan for 5 minutes. Serve warm, or transfer to a wire rack to cool.

banana maple muffins

makes 6 large muffins

Using bananas in a microwave muffin batter adds moisture that doesn't evaporate, ensuring that the muffins remain moist and well textured. This recipe has been written for a 650-watt microwave; if your oven uses a different wattage, adjust the cooking time accordingly.

MUFFINS

2 eggs

$1/3$ cup ($2^1/2$ oz/75 g) brown sugar

$1/3$ cup (3 oz/90 g) butter, cubed

2 small, ripe bananas

$1/3$ cup (3 fl oz/90 ml) maple syrup

$1/4$ teaspoon baking soda (bicarbonate of soda)

$1^1/2$ cups ($7^1/2$ oz/235 g) self-rising flour

GLAZE

1 cup (4 oz/125 g) confectioners' (icing) sugar

1 teaspoon unsweetened cocoa powder

$1/4$ cup (2 fl oz/60 ml) maple syrup

1–2 teaspoons water

chopped walnuts (optional)

✥ Using the chopping blade of a food processor or electric mixer, process eggs and sugar for 1 minute. With the motor still running, add the butter. Peel the bananas and drop them into the feed tube with the motor still running. Process until completely smooth. Add the maple syrup, baking soda, and flour in one pour (this is easier if the flour is first measured onto a sheet of paper). As soon as the flour is added, turn the motor off and scrape down the sides of the bowl. Pulse once or twice to complete mixing.

✥ Pour batter into six large (1-cup) microwave-safe muffin cups. Elevate cups from the oven floor, arranging them three at a time around the outside of the turntable. Cook on high (100%) until well risen and spongy to the touch, about 4 minutes. When cooked, stand in the cups for 5 minutes, loosely covered, then transfer to a wire rack to cool completely. Cook the remaining batter in the same way.

✥ For glaze, using the chopping blade of a food processor or electric mixer, process the confectioners' sugar and cocoa until mixed. With the motor running, gradually add the maple syrup, stopping when the glaze reaches a flowing consistency. If necessary, add some of the water. Using a tablespoon, pour the glaze over the top of the cooled muffins, allowing it to flow down the sides. Decorate top with chopped walnuts, if desired.

golden raisin–bran muffins

makes 12 standard muffins

Soaking the bran cereal in the liquid ingredients until fully plumped ensures that these muffins have a wonderfully moist texture. For best results, select an unprocessed bran cereal such as All Bran or Bran Buds.

2 eggs

⅓ cup (2½ oz/75 g) firmly packed light or dark brown sugar

½ cup (4 fl oz/125 ml) vegetable oil

2 cups (16 fl oz/500 ml) buttermilk

½ teaspoon salt

1½ cups (4 oz/125 g) wheat bran cereal (see note)

2¼ cups (11 oz/345 g) all-purpose (plain) flour

2 teaspoons baking soda (bicarbonate of soda)

1 cup (4 oz/125 g) golden raisins (sultanas)

❖ Preheat oven to 400°F (200°C). Grease twelve standard (½-cup) muffin cups or line them with parchment (baking) paper cases.

❖ In a large bowl, combine the eggs, brown sugar, vegetable oil, buttermilk, salt, and bran cereal. Using a wooden spoon, mix well. Let rest for at least 10 minutes and up to 1 hour to soften the bran.

❖ In another bowl, sift together the flour and baking soda. Add the flour mixture to the bran mixture, stirring until just combined. Do not overmix. Stir in the golden raisins.

❖ Spoon batter into prepared muffin cups, filling them two-thirds full. Bake until golden brown and a wooden skewer or toothpick inserted into the center of a muffin comes out clean, 15–20 minutes. Remove from oven and cool in pan for 5 minutes. Serve warm, or transfer to a wire rack to cool.

makes 6 large muffins

2 cups (10 oz/315 g)
self-rising flour

1/2 cup (4 oz/125 g) sugar

1/2 cup (3 1/2 oz/100 g)
semisweet (plain)
chocolate chips

1/2 cup (3 1/2 oz/100 g) sweet
(milk) chocolate chips

2 eggs, lightly beaten

1 cup (8 fl oz/250 ml) milk

1/3 cup (3 oz/90 g) butter,
melted

1 teaspoon vanilla extract
(essence)

CHOCOLATE GANACHE

3 oz (90 g) semisweet (plain)
chocolate, chopped

1/4 cup (2 fl oz/60 ml) heavy
(double) cream

1 1/2 tablespoons (3/4 oz/20 g)
butter

❖ Preheat oven to 400°F (200°C/Gas Mark 5). Grease six large (1-cup) muffin cups or line them with parchment (baking) paper cases.

❖ In a large mixing bowl, sift the flour. Stir through the sugar then add the chocolate chips. Make a well in the center.

❖ In a small mixing bowl, combine the eggs, milk, butter, and vanilla extract. Add all at once to the flour mixture and stir until just moistened (the batter should be lumpy).

❖ Spoon batter into prepared muffin cups, filling them two-thirds full. Bake until golden brown and a wooden skewer or toothpick inserted into the center of a muffin comes out clean, 25–30 minutes. Remove from oven and cool in pans for 5 minutes. Serve warm, or transfer to a wire rack to cool.

❖ For the ganache, place the chocolate, cream, and butter in a heatproof bowl over (not touching) a pan of simmering water. Stir gently over low heat until melted and smooth. Chill until firm, then pipe or spread ganache over the cooled muffins.

chocolate chip
muffins
with chocolate ganache

cranberry maple muffins

makes 12 standard muffins

1¾ cups (9 oz/280 g)
all-purpose (plain) flour

1½ teaspoons baking powder

¼ teaspoon baking soda
(bicarbonate of soda)

¼ teaspoon salt

1 egg, beaten

½ cup (4 fl oz/125 ml)
maple syrup

½ cup (4 fl oz/125 ml) milk

¼ cup (2 oz/60 g) butter, melted

½ cup (2 oz/60 g) dried cranberries
or cherries or chopped fresh
cranberries, or ½ cup (3 oz/90 g)
raisins, chopped

ICING

½ cup (2½ oz/75 g) confectioners'
(icing) sugar, sifted

¼ teaspoon maple flavoring or
vanilla extract (essence)

2–3 teaspoons milk

❖ Preheat oven to 400°F (200°C/Gas Mark 5). Grease twelve standard (½-cup) muffin cups or line with parchment (baking) paper cases.

❖ In a medium mixing bowl, sift together the flour, baking powder, baking soda, and salt. Make a well in the center.

❖ In a small mixing bowl, stir together the egg, maple syrup, milk, and butter. Add all at once to the flour mixture and stir until just moistened (the batter should be lumpy). Fold in the fruit.

❖ Spoon batter into prepared muffin cups, filling them two-thirds full. Bake until golden brown, about 15 minutes. Cool in pan for 5 minutes, then transfer to a wire rack.

❖ For the icing, in a small mixing bowl stir together the sifted confectioners' sugar, maple flavoring or vanilla, and enough milk to make a smooth icing of drizzling consistency. Drizzle over cooled muffins.

39

blueberry muffins

makes 12 standard muffins

2 cups (10 oz/315 g) self-rising flour

1/2 cup (4 oz/125 g) superfine (caster) sugar

1 egg, beaten

1 cup (8 fl oz/250 ml) milk

1/4 cup (2 oz/60 g) butter, melted

1 tablespoon grated orange zest

3/4 cup (6 oz/185 g) fresh or frozen blueberries

❖ Preheat oven to 400°F (200°C/Gas Mark 5). Grease twelve standard (1/2-cup) muffin cups or line them with parchment (baking) paper cases.

❖ In a large mixing bowl, sift the flour. Stir through the sugar. Make a well in the center.

❖ In another bowl, stir together the egg, milk, and butter. Add all at once to the flour mixture along with the orange zest and blueberries. Stir until just moistened (the mixture should be lumpy).

❖ Spoon batter into prepared pans, filling them two-thirds full. Bake until golden brown, about 15 minutes. Cool in pan for 5 minutes, then transfer to a wire rack.

passionfruit muffins
with glacé icing

makes 12 standard muffins

Note: this recipe requires about 6 passionfruit

2 cups (10 oz/315 g) self-rising flour

2/3 cup (5 1/2 oz/165 g) superfine (caster) sugar

2 eggs, lightly beaten

1/2 cup (4 fl oz/125 ml) milk

1/2 cup (2 oz/60 g) butter, melted

1/2 cup (4 1/2 fl oz/135 ml) passionfruit pulp

PASSIONFRUIT GLACÉ ICING

1 cup (5 oz/150 g) confectioners' (icing) sugar

3/4 oz (20 g) butter, melted

1–2 tablespoons passionfruit pulp

❖ Preheat oven to 400°F (200°C/Gas Mark 5). Grease twelve standard (½-cup) muffin cups or line them with parchment (baking) paper cases.

❖ In a large mixing bowl, sift the flour. Stir through the sugar. Make a well in the center.

❖ In a small mixing bowl, combine the eggs, milk, butter, and the ½ cup (4½ fl oz/135 ml) passionfruit pulp. Add all at once to the flour mixture and stir just until moistened (the batter should be lumpy).

❖ Spoon batter into prepared muffin cups, filling them two-thirds full. Bake until golden brown, 15–20 minutes. Cool in pan for 5 minutes, then transfer to a wire rack.

❖ For the icing, sift the confectioners' sugar into a small bowl. Add the ¾ oz (20 g) melted butter and enough of the passionfruit pulp to mix to a smooth and spreadable consistency. Spread the icing over the cooled muffins and allow to set before serving.

43

pumpkin muffins
with pumpkin seed crumble

makes 12 standard muffins

1 1/2 cups (7 oz/225 g)
self-rising flour

1/2 cup (3 oz/85 g) whole
wheat (wholemeal)
self-rising flour

1 teaspoon ground nutmeg

1/2 teaspoon baking soda
(bicarbonate of soda)

1/2 cup (3 oz/90 g) firmly
packed brown sugar

1 egg, lightly beaten

1/2 cup (4 fl oz/125 ml)
buttermilk

2 oz (60 g) butter, melted

1 cup (8 oz/250 g) cooked,
mashed pumpkin (see note)

PUMPKIN SEED CRUMBLE

1/4 cup (1 1/2 oz/40 g)
all-purpose (plain) flour

1 oz (30 g) cold butter,
chopped

1 tablespoon firmly packed
brown sugar

2 tablespoons pumpkin
seeds

❖ Preheat oven to 400°F (200°C/Gas Mark 5). Grease twelve standard (1/2-cup) muffin cups or line them with parchment (baking) paper cases.

❖ In a large mixing bowl, sift together the flours, nutmeg, and baking soda, returning the husks to the bowl. Stir through the brown sugar. Make a well in the center.

❖ In a small mixing bowl, stir together the egg, buttermilk, butter, and pumpkin. Add all at once to the flour mixture and stir until just moistened (the batter should be lumpy).

❖ Spoon batter into prepared muffin cups, filling them two-thirds full.

❖ For the crumble, place the flour in a small bowl and, using your fingertips, rub in the butter until the mixture is crumbly. Stir through the brown sugar and pumpkin seeds. Spoon topping evenly over muffins.

❖ Bake until golden brown and cooked through, 15–20 minutes. Remove from oven and cool in pan for 5 minutes. Serve warm, or transfer to a wire rack to cool.

❖ Note: To yield 1 cup (8 oz/250 g) mashed pumpkin, peel, seed, and cube 13 oz (400 g) pumpkin. Cook in the microwave or steam until tender. Cool, then mash.

sun-dried cherry, walnut, and sage muffins

makes 12 standard muffins

Muffins are infinitely adaptable to local and seasonal produce. Here, cherries and sage are imaginatively combined to satisfying effect.

2 cups (10 oz/315 g) self-rising flour

½ teaspoon baking powder

⅓ teaspoon salt

⅓ cup (3 oz/90 g) sugar

2 teaspoons finely chopped fresh sage

½ teaspoon ground cinnamon

¼ teaspoon ground nutmeg

2 eggs, lightly beaten

1 cup (8 fl oz/250 ml) milk

¼ cup (2 oz/60 g) unsalted butter, melted

1 tablespoon finely grated orange zest

¾ cup (3 oz/90 g) pitted sun-dried cherries

½ cup (2 oz/60 g) chopped walnuts

◈ Preheat oven to 400°F (200°C/Gas Mark 5). Grease twelve standard (½-cup) muffin cups or line them with parchment (baking) paper cases.

◈ In a medium mixing bowl, sift together the flour, baking powder, and salt. Stir through the sugar, sage, cinnamon, and nutmeg. Make a well in the center.

◈ In a small mixing bowl, combine the eggs, milk, and melted butter. Add all at once to the flour mixture and stir until just moistened (the batter should be lumpy). Add the orange zest, cherries, and walnuts. Stir briefly until just combined.

◈ Spoon batter into prepared muffin cups, filling them two-thirds full. Bake until golden brown and a wooden skewer or toothpick inserted into the center of a muffin comes out clean, 15–20 minutes. Remove from oven and cool in pan for 5 minutes. Serve warm, or transfer to a wire rack to cool.

making ahead

If desired, muffin batter may be frozen. Make a big batch, bake some straight away, and freeze the rest for later, as follows:

1. Grease pans and prepare batter as directed in recipe. Fill pans, adding any nut or crunch toppings.

2. Place unbaked pans of muffin batter into the freezer. When firm, transfer muffins to an airtight container or heavy-gauge, lock-top plastic bag and freeze for up to 4 weeks.

3. To bake, preheat oven and grease the same pan. Return frozen batter to cups and bake without thawing, allowing about 15 minutes extra cooking time.

apple and date muffins

makes 6 large muffins

Either fresh or dried dates
may be used in this recipe.
Fresh dates can be found all
year round, although their
peak season is from midfall
through midwinter. Choose
plump, shiny dates; avoid
any that are excessively
sticky or covered with
crystallized sugar.

MUFFINS

1 large green apple, peeled, cored, and finely chopped

1 cup (6 oz/185 g) chopped, pitted dates

1 teaspoon baking soda (bicarbonate of soda)

1 cup (8 fl oz/250 ml) boiling water

1/2 cup (4 oz/125 g) butter

3/4 cup (6 oz/185 g) granulated sugar

1 egg, lightly beaten

2 cups (10 oz/315 g) self-rising flour, sifted

TOPPING

1/4 cup (2 oz/60 g) butter

1/2 cup (3 1/2 oz/100 g) firmly packed brown sugar

1/2 cup (1 oz/30 g) shredded coconut

✧ Preheat oven to 375°F (190°C/Gas Mark 4). Grease six large (1-cup) muffin cups or line them with parchment (baking) paper cases.

✧ For muffins, combine the apples, dates, baking soda, and boiling water. Allow to cool.

✧ Using an electric mixer on medium to high speed, cream the butter and sugar until pale. Beat in the egg. Fold in the sifted flour alternately with the apple and date mixture. Spoon batter into prepared muffin cups.

✧ Bake for 15 minutes. Remove from oven and allow to cool slightly in pans while you make the topping.

✧ For topping, place butter, brown sugar, and coconut in a small saucepan and stir over moderate heat until the butter melts and the ingredients are combined.

✧ Spoon topping over muffins and return them to the oven. Bake until topping is bubbling and golden and a wooden skewer or toothpick inserted into the center of a muffin comes out clean, 5–8 minutes more. Serve warm, or transfer to a wire rack to cool.

muffin batters

There are two types of muffin batter. Some batters are made by adding all the liquid ingredients to the dry ones and mixing quickly. Others, like the recipe at left, are made like cakes, and call for butter and sugar to be creamed together, then dry and liquid ingredients to be added alternately. For the first type, the ingredients should be mixed quickly, with only a few stokes— just enough to combine the ingredients roughly. Any more stirring will develop the gluten in the flour, resulting in tough muffins.

lemon and caraway
muffins

makes 6 large or
12 standard muffins

Caraway, native to Europe
and Asia, is a member of the
parsley family. Its seeds have
a pungent, distinctive taste
and are used throughout
northern and central Europe
in baked goods, cheese-
making, savory dishes, and
liqueurs. Here, it is paired
with lemon, giving these
muffins a refreshing,
unusual flavor.

½ cup (4 oz/125 g) butter

¾ cup (6 oz/185 g) sugar

2 eggs

2 tablespoons grated lemon zest or
½ cup (3 oz/90 g) candied (glacé) lemon zest

1 tablespoon caraway seeds

⅔ cup (5½ fl oz/170 ml) milk

1 teaspoon vanilla extract (essence)

2 cups (10 oz/315 g) self-rising flour, sifted

◈ Preheat oven to 375°F (190°C/Gas Mark 4). Grease six large (1-cup) or twelve standard (½-cup) muffin cups or line them with parchment (baking) paper.

◈ Using an electric mixer on medium to high speed, cream the butter and sugar until light and fluffy. Add the eggs, one at a time, beating well after each addition. Stir in the lemon zest and caraway seeds.

◈ In a small measuring jug, combine the milk and vanilla extract.

◈ Fold the sifted flour into the butter-and-sugar mixture alternately with the milk and vanilla.

◈ Spoon batter into prepared muffin cups, filling them two-thirds full. Bake until golden brown and a wooden skewer or toothpick inserted into the center of a muffin comes out clean, 20–25 minutes for large muffins or 15–20 minutes for standard muffins. Remove from oven and cool in pan for 5 minutes. Serve warm, or transfer to a wire rack to cool.

pecan coffee muffins

makes 6 large muffins

$^1\!/_2$ cup (4 oz/125 g) butter, softened

$^3\!/_4$ cup (6 oz/185 g) sugar

2 eggs

2 teaspoons vanilla extract (essence)

2 cups (10 oz/315 g) all-purpose
(plain) flour

1 teaspoon baking powder

1 teaspoon baking soda
(bicarbonate of soda)

$^1\!/_2$ teaspoon salt

1 cup (8 fl oz/250 ml) light sour cream

FILLING

$^3\!/_4$ cup (5 oz/155 g) packed brown sugar

1 tablespoon ground cinnamon

1$^1\!/_2$ tablespoons unsweetened
cocoa powder

$^3\!/_4$ cup (4 oz/125 g) chopped raisins

$^3\!/_4$ cup (3 oz/90 g) chopped pecans

ICING

$^2\!/_3$ cup (5$^1\!/_2$ fl oz/170 ml) whipping cream

1 tablespoon strong black coffee

1–2 tablespoons confectioners'
(icing) sugar, sifted

✦ Preheat oven to 375°F (190°C/Gas Mark 4). Grease six large (1-cup) muffin cups or line them with parchment (baking) paper cases.

✦ For muffins, using an electric mixer on medium to high speed, cream the butter and sugar until light and fluffy. Beat in the eggs, one at a time, beating well after each addition. Beat in the vanilla. Sift together the flour, baking powder, baking soda, and salt. Fold in the sifted dry ingredients alternately with the sour cream, beginning and ending with the flour mixture.

✦ Spoon a third of the batter into the prepared muffin cups.

✦ For filling, in a small bowl, combine sugar, cinnamon, cocoa, raisins, and pecans. Mix well.

✦ Sprinkle half of the pecan filling evenly over the first layer of batter. Spoon half of the remaining batter on top of the filling. Sprinkle over the rest of the filling, then top with the remaining batter. Rap the pan on a hard surface several times to expel any bubbles.

✦ Bake until golden brown and a wooden skewer or toothpick inserted into the center of a muffin comes out clean, 20–25 minutes. Remove from oven, cool in pan for 5 minutes, then transfer to a wire rack. Allow to cool completely before icing.

✦ For icing, using an electric mixer on medium to high speed, whip the cream until soft peaks form. Fold in the coffee and then the sugar and mix well. Spread the icing over the top of the cooled muffins and serve.

chocolate cherry muffins

makes 6 large muffins

Cherries have an affinity with nuts, especially almonds. Ground almonds, as used in this recipe, or almond extract will enhance the flavor of the fruit.

2 cups (10 oz/315 g) self-rising flour

1 teaspoon ground allspice

¼ cup (1½ oz/45 g) ground almonds

⅓ cup (2½ oz/75 g) packed brown sugar

1 cup (5 oz/155 g) semisweet (plain) chocolate chips

1 cup (6 oz/185 g) bottled or canned sweet red cherries, pitted and drained, or 1 cup (6 oz/185 g) fresh sweet cherries, pitted

1 egg, lightly beaten

⅓ cup (3 oz/90 g) butter, melted

⅔ cup (5½ fl oz/170 ml) buttermilk

❖ Preheat oven to 400°F (200°C/Gas Mark 5). Grease six large (1-cup) muffin cups or line them with parchment (baking) paper.

❖ In a large mixing bowl, sift the flour and allspice. Stir through the ground almonds, sugar, chocolate chips, and cherries. Make a well in the center.

❖ In a small mixing bowl, combine the egg, butter, and buttermilk. Add all at once to the flour mixture and stir until just moistened (the batter will be lumpy).

❖ Spoon batter into prepared muffin cups, filling them two-thirds full. Bake until golden brown and a wooden skewer or toothpick inserted into the center of a muffin comes out clean, 20–25 minutes. Remove from oven and cool in pan for 5 minutes. Serve warm, or transfer to a wire rack to cool.

choosing cherries

Fresh, bottled, or canned sweet cherries may be used for this recipe. If using fresh cherries, choose plump, dark, smooth fruit with firm, green stems. Make sure they are ripe, as they will not ripen further off the tree. Avoid those that are hard and pale, indications of immature fruit, or those that are wet, sticky, bruised, very soft, or have shriveled stems, all signs of age. Where possible, always buy cherries with the stems attached; once the stems are removed, the fruit spoils more rapidly. Store cherries in a plastic bag in the refrigerator for up to 3 days.

date and apple microwave muffins

makes 6 large muffins

The apples and dates in this recipe help keep the muffins moist. This recipe is designed for a 650-watt microwave oven. If your oven uses a different wattage, adjust the cooking times accordingly. Test for doneness a minute or two before end of the stated cooking time; if necessary, return the muffins to the oven for a little longer.

1 cooking apple, peeled, cored, and coarsely grated

1 cup (6 oz/185 g) finely chopped pitted dates

⅓ cup (3 oz/90 g) butter, chopped

1 cup (8 fl oz/250 ml) very hot water

1 teaspoon baking soda (bicarbonate of soda)

¾ cup (6 oz/185 g) superfine (caster) sugar

1 egg

1 teaspoon vanilla extract (essence)

1½ cups (7½ oz/235 g) self-rising flour

¼ teaspoon salt

◈ Place apple, dates, butter, and water in a large microwave-safe mixing bowl and heat on high (100%) for 1 minute. Quickly stir through the baking soda and sugar and set aside until well cooled but not cold.

◈ When the mixture is cool, add the egg and vanilla and whisk well. Sift the flour and salt over the mixture and mix well. Do not overmix.

◈ Pour batter into six large (1-cup) microwave-safe muffin cups. Elevate cups from the oven floor, arranging them three at a time around the outside of the turntable. Cook on high (100%) until well risen and spongy to the touch, about 4 minutes. When cooked, remove from oven and let stand in the cups for 5 minutes, loosely covered. Serve warm, or transfer to a wire rack to cool. Cook the remaining batter in the same way.

recipe variations

Serve warm with custard for dessert.

....

Scatter ½ cup (2 oz/60 g) chopped nuts of your choice over the base of microwave-safe muffin cups before adding the mixture.

....

Replace the vanilla with 1–2 teaspoons grated lemon or orange zest, or add 1 teaspoon mixed spice.

chocolate, ginger, and walnut muffins

makes 6 large muffins

¼ cup (2 fl oz/60 ml) heavy
(double) cream

6½ oz (200 g) semisweet (plain) chocolate

⅓ cup (3 oz/90 g) butter

2 eggs

¾ cup (6 oz/185 g) granulated (white) sugar

2 cups (10 oz/315 g) self-rising flour, sifted

½ teaspoon baking soda (bicarbonate
of soda)

⅓ cup (2½ oz/75 g) chopped candied
(glacé) ginger

¾ cup (3 oz/90 g) chopped walnuts

ICING

1½ oz (45 g) chopped candied (glacé)
ginger

1 tablespoon rum

½ cup (3 oz/90 g) firmly packed
brown sugar

½ cup (4 fl oz/125 ml) heavy
(double) cream

2 tablespoons (1 oz/30 g) butter

*Extra chopped candied (glacé) ginger,
to decorate (optional)*

◈ Preheat oven to 375°F (190°C/Gas Mark 4). Grease six large (1-cup) muffin cups or line them with parchment (baking) paper cases.

◈ Combine the cream and chocolate in the top of a double boiler and stir over (not touching) simmering water until combined. Stir in the butter and set aside to cool.

◈ In a medium mixing bowl, using an electric mixer on medium to high speed, beat the eggs and granulated sugar until pale. Stir into the chocolate mixture alternately with the sifted flour, baking soda, ginger, and walnuts.

◈ Spoon batter into prepared muffin cups, filling them two-thirds full. Bake until golden brown and a wooden skewer or toothpick inserted into the center of a muffin comes out clean, 20–25 minutes. Remove from oven, cool in pan for 5 minutes, and transfer to a wire rack. Allow to cool completely before icing.

◈ For icing, in a small bowl, combine the ginger and rum and allow to soak for 10 minutes. In a small saucepan, combine the sugar and one-third of the cream. Bring to a boil, stirring frequently, then reduce the heat and simmer for 10 minutes. Remove from heat and whisk in the ginger and rum mixture and the butter. Refrigerate for 10 minutes.

◈ Using an electric mixer on medium to high speed, beat the remaining cream until soft peaks form. Gently fold into the cooled mixture and spread over the muffins. Decorate with the extra chopped ginger, if desired.

banana and chocolate chip muffins

makes 12 standard muffins

Mashed bananas add moisture and flavor to these muffins. Use very ripe bananas, with skins well splotched with black, as they will be softer and sweeter. Mash them with a fork, adding a few drops of lemon juice, if you wish, to prevent the fruit from browning.

2 cups (10 oz/315 g) self-rising flour

1/2 teaspoon baking soda (bicarbonate of soda)

1/2 cup (4 oz/125 g) sugar

1 cup (7 oz/210 g) semisweet (plain) chocolate chips

2 eggs, lightly beaten

1/2 cup (4 fl oz/125 ml) milk

1/4 cup (2 oz/60 g) butter, melted

2 medium bananas, mashed (to yield about 1 cup/ 8 oz/250 g)

❖ Preheat oven to 400°F (200°C/Gas Mark 5). Grease twelve standard (½-cup) muffin cups or line them with parchment (baking) paper cases.

❖ In a large mixing bowl, sift together the self-rising flour and baking soda. Stir in the sugar and ½ cup (3½ oz/100 g) of the chocolate chips. Make a well in the center.

❖ In a small mixing bowl, combine the eggs, milk, melted butter, and mashed banana. Add all at once to the flour mixture and stir until just moistened (the batter should be lumpy).

❖ Spoon batter into prepared muffin cups, filling them two-thirds full. Sprinkle with the remaining ½ cup (3½ oz/100 g) chocolate chips.

❖ Bake until golden brown and a wooden skewer or toothpick inserted into the center of a muffin comes out clean, 15–20 minutes. Remove from oven and cool in pan for 5 minutes. Serve warm, or transfer to a wire rack to cool.

apple muffins
with crumble topping

makes 12 standard muffins

Apples that hold their shape
during cooking are the best
choice for this recipe.
Suitable varieties include
Golden Delicious, Granny
Smith, Honeycrisp, Jonathan,
Pippin, and York.

2 cups (10 oz/315 g) self-rising flour

1 teaspoon ground cinnamon

½ cup (3 oz/90 g) firmly packed brown sugar

1 large apple, peeled, cored, and chopped

½ cup (2 oz/60 g) golden raisins (sultanas)

2 eggs, lightly beaten

1 cup (8 fl oz/250 ml) apple juice

2 oz (60 g) butter, melted

CRUMBLE TOPPING

2 tablespoons (1 oz/30 g) butter, chopped

¼ cup (1¼ oz/40 g) all-purpose (plain) flour

1 tablespoon firmly packed brown sugar

1 tablespoon pumpkin seeds (pepitas)

◈ Preheat oven to 400°F (200°C/Gas Mark 5). Grease twelve standard (½-cup) muffin cups or line them with parchment (baking) paper cases.

◈ In a large mixing bowl, sift together the self-rising flour and cinnamon. Stir through the brown sugar, chopped apple, and golden raisins. Make a well in the center.

◈ In a small mixing bowl, combine the eggs, apple juice, and butter. Add all at once to the flour mixture and stir until just moistened (the batter should be lumpy).

◈ Spoon batter into prepared muffin cups, filling them two-thirds full.

◈ For the crumble topping, in a small bowl, rub the chopped butter into the flour until it looks crumbly. Stir in the brown sugar and pumpkin seeds. Spoon topping evenly over the muffins.

◈ Bake until golden brown and a wooden skewer or toothpick inserted into the center of a muffin comes out clean, 15–20 minutes. Remove from oven and cool in pan for 5 minutes. Serve warm, or transfer to a wire rack to cool.

marmalade poppyseed muffins

makes 12 standard muffins

Marmalade performs a dual function in these muffins, adding tang and giving the tops a pleasing glaze. Experiment with different flavors of marmalade to see which you like best.

¼ cup (2 oz/60 g) butter, chopped

⅔ cup (7 oz/210 g) marmalade

2 cups (10 oz/315 g) self-rising flour

½ teaspoon baking powder

⅓ cup (1¾ oz/50 g) poppy seeds

½ cup (4 oz/125 g) sugar

2 eggs, lightly beaten

¾ cup (6 fl oz/185 ml) milk

2 teaspoons finely grated lemon zest

2 teaspoons finely grated orange zest

✦ Preheat oven to 400°F (200°C/Gas Mark 5). Grease twelve standard (½-cup) muffin cups or line them with parchment (baking) paper cases.

✦ In a small saucepan over low heat, melt the butter and ⅓ cup (3½ oz/105 g) of the marmalade. Stir with a fork to combine. Set aside to cool.

✦ In a large mixing bowl, sift together the self-rising flour and baking powder. Stir through the poppy seeds and sugar. Make a well in the center.

✦ In a small mixing bowl, combine the eggs, milk, lemon and orange zests, and butter and marmalade mixture. Add all at once to flour mixture and stir until just moistened (the batter should be lumpy).

✦ Spoon batter into prepared muffin cups, filling them two-thirds full.

✦ Bake until golden brown and a wooden skewer or toothpick inserted into the center of a muffin comes out clean, 15–20 minutes. Remove from oven and leave in pan while you make the glaze.

✦ In a small saucepan over low heat, gently melt the remaining ⅓ cup (3½ oz/105 g) of the marmalade. Push it through a fine sieve; discard the contents of the sieve. Using a pastry brush, brush the hot marmalade over the hot muffins. Serve warm, or transfer to a wire rack to cool.

pecan and sour cream muffins

makes 8–10 standard muffins

These muffins owe their velvety texture to sour cream or its close relation crème fraîche. Crème fraîche, originally from France, is a soured, cultured cream product with a tangy flavor and thick, silken texture. It is available from gourmet markets, cheese shops, and some supermarkets. You can also make your own (see box, page 67).

MUFFINS

¾ cup (6 oz/185 g) granulated (white) sugar

⅔ cup (5 oz/155 g) butter, chopped into small pieces

1 teaspoon vanilla extract (essence)

2 eggs

2 cups (10 oz/315 g) self-rising flour, sifted

½ teaspoon baking soda (bicarbonate of soda)

1 cup (8 fl oz/250 ml) sour cream or crème fraîche

FILLING

1 cup (4 oz/125 g) chopped pecans

1 teaspoon ground cinnamon

2 tablespoons (1 oz/30 g) firmly packed brown sugar

Melted butter, for glazing (optional)

◈ Preheat oven to 375°F (190°C/Gas Mark 4). Grease twelve standard (½-cup) muffin cups or line them with parchment (baking) paper.

◈ In a food processor, combine the granulated sugar, butter, vanilla, eggs, flour, baking soda, and sour cream or crème fraîche. Process until smooth, 1–2 minutes.

◈ Pour half of the batter into prepared muffin cups.

◈ In a small bowl, combine the pecans, cinnamon, and brown sugar and sprinkle half over the mixture in the pan. Top with the remaining batter, then sprinkle with the remaining pecan and sugar mixture.

◈ Bake until golden brown and a wooden skewer or toothpick inserted into the middle of a muffin comes out clean, 15–20 minutes. Remove from oven and cool in the pan for 5 minutes. Serve warm, or transfer to a wire rack to cool. If desired, brush the muffins with a little melted butter.

recipe hint

To make 1 cup (8 fl oz/ 250 ml) crème fraîche:

1. Combine 1 cup (8 fl oz/ 250 ml) heavy (double) cream and 1 tablespoon buttermilk in a small saucepan over low heat. Heat to lukewarm. Do not allow to simmer.

2. Remove from heat, cover, and allow to thicken at warm room temperature. This can take from 8 to 48 hours, depending on your taste and recipe needs.

3. Once the mixture is as thick and flavorful as you want, refrigerate until well chilled before using.

4. Store, covered, in the refrigerator for up to 1 week.

dried apricot and apple muffins

makes 12 standard muffins

Chewy dried fruits combine with the tang of citrus in these delicious muffins. A simple almond-and-sugar topping adds crunch and visual appeal.

½ cup (3 oz/90 g) chopped dried apricots

½ cup (1½ oz/45 g) chopped dried apple

½ cup (4 fl oz/125 ml) orange juice

2 cups (10 oz/315 g) self-rising flour

½ cup (3½ oz/105 g) brown sugar

2 eggs, lightly beaten

1 cup (8 fl oz/250 ml) buttermilk

¼ cup (2 oz/60 g) butter, melted

1 teaspoon grated orange zest

TOPPING

½ cup (2 oz/60 g) slivered almonds

⅓ cup (2½ oz/75 g) demerara sugar

❧ Preheat oven to 400°F (200°C/Gas Mark 5). Generously butter twelve standard (½-cup) muffin cups or line them with parchment (baking) paper cases.

❧ In a small bowl, combine the chopped dried fruit and the orange juice. Leave to soak for 15 minutes.

❧ In a large mixing bowl, sift the flour. Stir through the brown sugar. Make a well in the center.

❧ In a small mixing bowl, combine the eggs, buttermilk, butter, and orange zest. Add all at once to the flour mixture, together with the soaked dried fruit and orange juice. Stir until just moistened (the batter should be lumpy).

❧ Spoon batter into prepared muffin cups, filling them two-thirds full. Scatter the slivered almonds and demerara sugar over the muffins.

❧ Bake until golden brown and a wooden skewer or toothpick inserted into the center of a muffin comes out clean, 15–20 minutes. Remove from oven, cool in pan for 5 minutes. Serve warm, or transfer to a wire rack to cool.

strawberry cheesecake
muffins

makes 6 large muffins

These muffins contain a
double hit of delicious
strawberries, as well as a
hidden surprise: a cube of
cream cheese in the center.

2 cups (10 oz/315 g) self-rising flour

½ cup (4 oz/125 g) granulated (white) sugar

1 cup (6 oz/175 g) chopped fresh strawberries

2 eggs, lightly beaten

1 cup (8 fl oz/250 ml) milk

2 oz (60 g) butter, melted

¼ cup (2¾ oz/80 g) strawberry jam

1 teaspoon vanilla extract (essence)

2 oz (60 g) cream cheese, cut into 6 cubes

1 tablespoon strawberry jam, extra

confectioners' (icing) sugar, for dusting

◈ Preheat oven to 400°F (200°C/Gas Mark 5).
Grease six large (1-cup) muffin cups or line them with
parchment (baking) paper cases.

◈ In a large mixing bowl, sift the self-rising flour.
Stir through the granulated sugar, then add the
chopped strawberries. Make a well in the center.

◈ In a small mixing bowl, combine the eggs, milk,
butter, jam, and vanilla extract. Add all at once to the
flour mixture and stir until just moistened (the batter
should be lumpy).

◈ Spoon two-thirds of the batter into prepared muffin
cups. Place a cube of cream cheese into the center of
each cup and top with a little of the extra jam. Cover
with the remaining batter.

◈ Bake until golden brown and a wooden skewer or
toothpick inserted into the center of a muffin comes
out clean, 25–30 minutes. Remove from oven and
cool in pan for 5 minutes. Serve warm, dusted with
confectioners' sugar.

recipe hint

After chopping the straw-
berries, gently wipe the pieces
with paper towel to soak up
excess juice and prevent it
from coloring the batter.

date and oat bran muffins

makes 12 standard muffins

Oat bran is less fibrous than wheat bran and has a subtly nutty flavor, which may come as a pleasant surprise to those who don't usually care for bran. Along with dates, it helps give these muffins a good measure of fiber. The inclusion of soy milk makes this recipe suitable for those who can't tolerate cow's milk.

2 oz (60 g) butter, chopped

1/4 cup (3 fl oz/90 ml) light molasses (golden syrup)

1 1/2 cups (7 oz/225 g) self-rising flour

1/2 teaspoon baking soda (bicarbonate of soda)

1 cup (5 oz/150 g) oat bran

1/3 cup (2 1/4 oz/65 g) brown sugar

1 cup (6 oz/180 g) chopped pitted dried or fresh dates

2 eggs, lightly beaten

1 cup (8 fl oz/250 ml) soy milk

✧ Preheat oven to 400°F (200°C/Gas Mark 5). Grease twelve standard (½-cup) muffin cups or line them with parchment (baking) paper cases.

✧ In a small saucepan over low heat, melt the butter and light molasses. Set aside to cool.

✧ In a large mixing bowl, sift together the self-rising flour and baking soda. Stir through the oat bran, brown sugar, and dates. Make a well in the center.

✧ Add the beaten eggs and soy milk to the cooled butter and golden syrup mixture. Add all at once to the flour mixture and stir until just moistened (the batter should be lumpy).

✧ Spoon batter into prepared muffin cups, filling them two-thirds full.

✧ Bake until golden brown and a wooden skewer or toothpick inserted into the center of a muffin comes out clean, 15–20 minutes. Remove from oven and cool in pan for 5 minutes. Serve warm, or transfer to a wire rack to cool.

gingerbread pear muffins

makes 6 large muffins

MUFFINS

2 oz (60 g) butter

⅓ cup (4 fl oz/115 ml) light molasses (golden syrup)

1½ cups (7 oz/225 g) self-rising flour

¾ cup (4½ oz/130 g) whole wheat (wholemeal) all-purpose (plain) flour

1½ tablespoons ground ginger

½ teaspoon baking soda (bicarbonate of soda)

⅓ cup (2¼ oz/65 g) brown sugar

2 eggs, lightly beaten

1 cup (8 fl oz/250 ml) milk

¼ cup (2 oz/60 g) chopped candied (glacé) ginger

1 large pear, peeled, cored, and chopped

GINGER GLACÉ ICING

1¾ oz (50 g) butter

1 teaspoon light molasses (golden syrup)

1 cup (5 oz/150 g) confectioners' (icing) sugar, sifted

1 teaspoon ground ginger

⅓ cup (2½ oz/75 g) chopped candied (glacé) ginger, extra

◈ Preheat oven to 400°F (200°C/Gas Mark 5). Grease six large (1-cup) muffin cups or line them with parchment (baking) paper cases.

◈ For muffins, in a small saucepan over low heat, gently melt the butter and light molasses. Stir to combine, then set aside to cool.

◈ In a large mixing bowl, sift together the flours, ground ginger, and baking soda, returning the husks to the bowl. Stir through the brown sugar. Make a well in the center.

◈ In a small mixing bowl, combine the eggs, milk, and the cooled butter and molasses mixture. Add all at once to the flour mixture together with the crystallized ginger and chopped pear. Stir until just moistened (the batter should be lumpy).

◈ Spoon batter into prepared muffin cups, filling them two-thirds full.

◈ Bake until golden brown and a wooden skewer or toothpick inserted into the center of a muffin comes out clean, 25–30 minutes. Remove from oven and cool in pan for 5 minutes. Transfer to a wire rack and allow to cool completely before icing.

◈ For icing, in a small saucepan over low heat, melt the butter and light molasses. Add the confectioners' sugar and ground ginger and stir over a low heat until melted and smooth. Spread the warm icing over the cooled muffins and sprinkle with the extra chopped ginger.

whole wheat banana
muffins
with nutty streusel topping

1 1/2 cups (8 oz/250 g) whole wheat
(wholemeal) self-rising flour

3/4 cup (4 oz/125 g) self-rising flour

1 teaspoon mixed spice

1/2 teaspoon baking soda
(bicarbonate of soda)

1/2 cup (3 oz/90 g) dark brown sugar

1 egg, lightly beaten

1/2 cup (4 fl oz/125 ml) milk

1/4 cup (2 oz/60 g) butter, melted

2 medium bananas, mashed, to yield about
1 cup (8 oz/250 g)

NUTTY STREUSEL TOPPING

2 tablespoons all-purpose (plain) flour

2 tablespoons raw sugar

1/2 teaspoon mixed spice

1/3 cup (1 1/2 oz/40 g) chopped pecans

1 oz (30 g) butter, melted

❖ Preheat oven to 400°F (200°C/Gas Mark 5). Grease twelve standard (½-cup) muffin cups or line them with parchment (baking) paper cases.

❖ In a large mixing bowl, sift together the flours, mixed spice, and baking soda, returning the husks to the bowl. Stir through the brown sugar. Make a well in the center.

❖ In a small mixing bowl, combine the egg, milk, butter, and banana. Add all at once to the flour mixture and stir until just moistened (the batter should be lumpy).

❖ Spoon batter into prepared muffin cups, filling them two-thirds full.

❖ For the topping, in a small bowl combine the flour, raw sugar, mixed spice, and pecans. Add the butter and stir to moisten the dry ingredients. Spoon the topping evenly over the muffins.

❖ Bake until golden brown and a wooden skewer or toothpick inserted into the center of a muffin comes out clean, 15–20 minutes. Remove from oven and cool in pan for 5 minutes. Serve warm, or transfer to a wire rack to cool.

fig and bran muffins

makes 12 standard muffins

Dried figs are often sold in blocks or rounds, but they will lose their shape if packed too tightly. It is preferable to buy dried figs in bulk at health-food stores or specialty markets. Dried figs should still be slightly soft. Keep them in a cool, dry place for 1–2 months, or in a plastic bag or airtight container in the refrigerator for up to 6 months.

1 cup (2½ oz/75 g) unprocessed bran

1¼ cups (10 fl oz/315 ml) milk

¼ cup (2 oz/60 g) butter

¼ cup (3 fl oz/90 ml) light molasses (golden syrup)

1½ cups (7 oz/225 g) self-rising flour

1 teaspoon baking powder

½ cup (3 oz/90 g) chopped dried figs

⅓ cup (2¼ oz/65 g) brown sugar

2 eggs, lightly beaten

3 dried figs, extra, each cut into 4 slices

❖ Preheat oven to 400°F (200°C/Gas Mark 5). Grease twelve standard (½-cup) muffin cups or line them with parchment (baking) paper cases.

❖ In a medium bowl, combine the bran and milk. Set aside for 15 minutes to soften.

❖ In a small saucepan over low heat, melt the butter and light molasses. Set aside to cool.

❖ In a large mixing bowl, sift together the flour and baking powder. Stir through the chopped figs and brown sugar. Make a well in the center.

❖ Add the eggs to the bran and milk mixture. Add all at once to the flour mixture together with the butter and light molasses. Stir until just moistened (the batter should be lumpy).

❖ Spoon batter into prepared muffin cups, filling them two-thirds full. Place a fig slice on the top of each muffin.

❖ Bake until golden brown and a wooden skewer or toothpick inserted into the center of a muffin comes out clean, 15–20 minutes. Remove from oven and cool in pan for 5 minutes. Serve warm, or transfer to a wire rack to cool.

makes 6 large muffins

*½ cup (1½ oz/45 g) chopped
dried apples*

½ cup (4 fl oz/125 ml) apple juice

*1½ cups (7 oz/225 g) self-rising
flour*

*½ cup (3 oz/85 g) whole wheat
(wholemeal) self-rising flour*

½ teaspoon baking powder

*⅓ cup (2¼ oz/65 g) firmly packed
brown sugar*

*1 cup (4½ oz/135 g) toasted
muesli*

1 egg, lightly beaten

1 cup (8 fl oz/250 ml) soy milk

2 oz (60 g) butter, melted

MUESLI CRUMBLE TOPPING

*⅓ cup (1½ oz/45 g) toasted
muesli*

*⅓ cup (2¼ oz/65 g) firmly packed
brown sugar*

*1 tablespoon all-purpose
(plain) flour*

*2 tablespoons (1 oz/30 g)
melted butter*

✧ Preheat oven to 400°F (200°C/Gas Mark 5). Grease six large (1-cup) muffin cups or line them with parchment (baking) paper cases.

✧ Place apple and apple juice in a small bowl and set aside for 15 minutes to soften slightly.

✧ In a large mixing bowl, sift together the flours and baking powder, returning the husks to the bowl. Stir through the brown sugar and muesli. Make a well in the center.

✧ In a small mixing bowl, combine the egg, soy milk, and butter. Add all at once to the flour mixture, together with the soaked apple and the apple juice. Stir until just moistened (the batter should be lumpy). Spoon batter into prepared pans, filling them two-thirds full.

✧ For the topping, in a small bowl combine the muesli, brown sugar, and flour. Add the butter and stir to moisten the dry ingredients. Spoon the topping evenly over the muffins.

✧ Bake until golden brown, 25–30 minutes. Cool in pans for 5 minutes, then transfer to a wire rack.

muesli and apple muffins

triple chocolate muffins

makes 12 standard muffins

2 cups (10 oz/315g) self-rising flour

½ teaspoon baking soda (bicarbonate of soda)

⅓ cup (1¼ oz/40 g) unsweetened
cocoa powder

½ cup (4 oz/125 g) sugar

½ cup (3½ oz/100 g) semisweet
(plain) chocolate chips

½ cup (3½ oz/100 g) sweet (milk)
chocolate chips

2 eggs, lightly beaten

1½ cups (12 fl oz/375 ml)
milk

¼ cup (2 oz/60 g)
butter, melted

CHOCOLATE ICING

½ cup (3½ oz/105 g) semisweet
(plain) chocolate chips

82

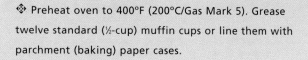

❖ Preheat oven to 400°F (200°C/Gas Mark 5). Grease twelve standard (½-cup) muffin cups or line them with parchment (baking) paper cases.

❖ In a large mixing bowl, sift together the flour, baking soda, and cocoa. Stir through the sugar and chocolate chips. Make a well in the center.

❖ In a small mixing bowl, combine the eggs, milk, and butter. Add all at once to the flour mixture and stir until just moistened (the batter should be lumpy).

❖ Spoon batter into prepared muffin cups, filling them two-thirds full. Bake until a wooden skewer or toothpick inserted into the center of a muffin comes out clean, 15–20 minutes. Remove from oven, cool in pan for 5 minutes, then transfer to a wire rack.

❖ For the chocolate icing, place the chocolate chips in a microwave-safe bowl and melt in short bursts in the microwave. Stir until smooth. (Or, place the chocolate chips in a heatproof bowl and sit the bowl over a pan of simmering water. Stir until melted and smooth.) Using a teaspoon, swirl the icing thickly over the tops of the cooled muffins.

83

cherry muffins
with white chocolate drizzle

makes 12 standard muffins

2 cups (10 oz/315 g) self-rising flour

½ cup (4 oz/125 g) sugar

2 eggs, lightly beaten

1 cup (8 fl oz/250 ml) milk

⅓ cup (3 oz/90 g) butter, melted

1 teaspoon vanilla essence (extract)

14 oz (425 g) can pitted black cherries, well drained

3 oz (90 g) white chocolate, chopped

❖ Preheat oven to 400°F (200°C/Gas Mark 5). Grease twelve standard (½-cup) muffin cups or line them with parchment (baking) paper cases.

❖ In a large mixing bowl, sift the flour. Stir through the sugar. Make a well in the center.

❖ In a small mixing bowl, combine the eggs, milk, butter, and vanilla. Add all at once to the flour mixture together with the cherries and stir until just moistened (the batter should be lumpy).

❖ Spoon batter into prepared cups, filling them two-thirds full. Bake until golden brown, 15–20 minutes. Cool in pan for 5 minutes, then transfer to a wire rack. Allow to cool before icing.

❖ For drizzle, place chopped chocolate in a plastic bag and melt in short bursts in the microwave. Alternatively, place chocolate in a heatproof bowl and sit bowl over a pan of simmering water. Stir until melted and smooth, then pour into a plastic bag. Snip a small piece off one corner of the bag and drizzle the chocolate over the cooled muffins.

lemon poppyseed muffins

makes 12 standard muffins

2 cups (10 oz/315 g) self-rising flour

1/4 teaspoon salt

1 1/2 tablespoons poppyseeds

3/4 cup (6 oz/185 g) granulated
(white) sugar

2 eggs

1/2 cup (4 fl oz/125 ml) milk

1/2 cup (4 oz/125 g) butter,
at room temperature

1 1/2 teaspoons vanilla extract
(essence)

grated zest of 1 lemon

❖ Preheat oven to 375°F (190°C/Gas Mark 4).
Grease twelve standard (½-cup) muffin cups or
line them with parchment (baking) paper cases.

❖ In a large mixing bowl, sift the flour and salt.
Stir in the poppyseeds and sugar. Make a well
in the center.

❖ In a small mixing bowl, combine the eggs, milk,
butter, vanilla, and lemon zest. Add all at once
to the flour mixture and stir until just moistened
(the batter should be lumpy).

❖ Spoon batter into prepared muffin cups, filling
them two-thirds full. Bake until golden brown and
cooked when tested with a skewer, 15–20 minutes.
Cool in pan for 5 minutes. Serve warm, or transfer
to a wire rack to cool.

❖ Note: If you prefer, you can make six large
(1-cup) muffins instead. Increase cooking time
to 20–25 minutes.

honey and spice
muffins
with almond-sugar cube topping

makes 12 standard muffins

¼ cup (2 oz/60 g) butter

⅓ cup (4 fl oz/115 ml) honey

*2 cups (10 oz/315 g)
self-rising flour*

½ teaspoon baking powder

1 teaspoon ground cinnamon

1 teaspoon ground ginger

1 teaspoon mixed spice

1 teaspoon ground cardamom

125 g slivered almonds

2 eggs, lightly beaten

¾ cup (6 fl oz/185 ml) milk

ALMOND–SUGAR CUBE
TOPPING

*⅔ cup (3 oz/85 g)
slivered almonds*

*12 sugar cubes,
roughly crushed*

❖ Preheat an oven to 400°F (200°C/Gas Mark 5). Generously butter twelve standard (½-cup) muffin tins or line with parchment (baking) paper cases.

❖ In a small saucepan, melt the butter and honey together over low heat. Set aside to cool.

❖ Sift together the flour, baking powder, and spices into a large mixing bowl.

❖ In a food processor, finely grind the slivered almonds. Stir the ground almonds through the dry ingredients. Make a well in the center.

❖ In a small mixing bowl combine the eggs, milk, and butter and honey mixture. Add all at once to the flour mixture and stir until just moistened (the batter should be lumpy).

❖ Spoon batter into the prepared tins, filling each tin two-thirds full.

❖ Sprinkle muffin tops with the slivered almonds and crushed sugar cubes, lightly pressing into the batter.

❖ Bake until golden brown, 15–20 minutes. Cool in pan for 5 minutes. Serve warm, or transfer to a wire rack to cool.

semolina muffins
with orange syrup

2 cups (10 oz/315 g) self-rising flour

½ teaspoon baking powder

1 cup (4 oz/125 g) fine semolina

½ cup (4 oz/125 g) sugar

2 eggs, lightly beaten

1 cup (8 fl oz/250 ml) milk

¼ cup (2 oz/60 g) butter, melted

2 teaspoons grated orange zest

½ cup (4 fl oz/125 ml) orange juice

ORANGE SYRUP

½ cup (4 oz/125 g) sugar

finely shredded zest of 1 small orange

½ cup (4 fl oz/125 ml) orange juice

½ cup (4 fl oz/125 ml) water

◈ Preheat oven to 400°F (200°C/Gas Mark 5). Grease twelve standard (½-cup) muffin cups or line them with parchment (baking) paper cases.

◈ In a large mixing bowl, sift together the self-rising flour and baking powder. Stir through the semolina and sugar. Make a well in the center.

◈ In a small mixing bowl, combine the eggs, milk, butter, orange zest, and juice. Add all at once to the flour mixture and stir until just moistened (the batter should be lumpy).

◈ Spoon batter into prepared muffin cups, filling them two-thirds full. Bake until golden brown and a wooden skewer or toothpick inserted into the center of a muffin comes out clean, 15–20 minutes.

◈ Meanwhile, make the orange syrup: Place the sugar, orange zest, orange juice, and water in a small saucepan. Stir over a low heat, without boiling, until the sugar has dissolved. Bring to the boil and simmer until syrupy and reduced by about one third, about 10 minutes.

◈ Remove pan from oven; do not remove muffins from cups. While still hot, prick the muffins all over with a fine skewer. Pour over the hot syrup. Set aside to cool a little and soak up the syrup before removing from the muffin cups. Serve warm, or transfer to a wire rack to cool.

date and pecan muffins
with butterscotch sauce

makes 12 standard muffins

1 cup (6 oz/185 g) chopped dates

3/4 cup (4 1/2 oz/140 g) brown sugar

1/2 cup (4 oz/125 g) butter

1 1/4 cups (10 fl oz/315 ml) water

1 teaspoon baking soda
(bicarbonate of soda)

1 teaspoon vanilla extract (essence)

1 1/2 cups (7 oz/225 g) self-rising flour

1/2 cup (3 oz/85 g) whole wheat
(wholemeal) all-purpose (plain) flour

1/2 cup (2 oz/60 g) pecans, chopped

2 eggs, lightly beaten

BUTTERSCOTCH SAUCE

1/2 cup (3 oz/90 g) brown sugar

1/4 cup (2 oz/60 g) butter

1/2 cup (4 fl oz/125 ml) heavy (double)
cream

✧ Preheat oven to 400°F (200°C/Gas Mark 5). Grease twelve standard (½-cup) muffin cups or line them with parchment (baking) paper cases.

✧ Place the dates, brown sugar, butter, and water in a medium saucepan. Stir over low heat until the butter has melted. Bring to the boil, still over low heat, and boil for 2 minutes. Remove from heat, cool slightly, then stir in the baking soda and vanilla. Set aside to cool.

✧ In a large mixing bowl, sift together the flours, returning the husks to the bowl. Stir through the pecans. Make a well in the center.

✧ Add the beaten eggs to the date mixture. Add all at once to the flour mixture and stir until just moistened (the batter should be lumpy).

✧ Spoon batter into prepared muffin cups, filling them two-thirds full. Bake until golden brown and a wooden skewer or toothpick inserted into the center of a muffin comes out clean, 15–20 minutes.

✧ Meanwhile, make the butterscotch sauce. Place the brown sugar, butter, and cream in a small saucepan. Stir over a low heat until the sugar has dissolved. Bring to a low boil and boil for 1 minute.

✧ Remove muffins from oven. Cool in pan for 5 minutes, then brush muffins with a little of the sauce. Remove from pan and serve warm with the remaining hot butterscotch sauce.

raspberry and white chocolate muffins

makes 12 standard muffins

The tang of raspberries provides a delicious counterpoint for the creamy richness of the white chocolate in these decadent muffins. If using frozen raspberries, there is no need to thaw them first.

1 cup (6 oz/175 g) white chocolate chips

¼ cup (2 oz/60 g) butter

2 cups (10 oz/315 g) self-rising flour

½ cup (4 oz/125 g) sugar

2 eggs, lightly beaten

1 cup (8 fl oz/250 ml) milk

1½ cups (6 oz/185 g) fresh or frozen raspberries

confectioners' (icing) sugar, for dusting

◈ Preheat oven to 400°F (200°C/Gas Mark 5). Grease twelve standard (½-cup) muffin cups or line them with parchment (baking) paper cases.

◈ In a small saucepan over low heat, melt half the chocolate chips and the butter, stirring gently until smooth. Set aside to cool.

◈ In a large mixing bowl, sift the flour. Stir through the sugar and the remaining chocolate chips. Make a well in the center.

◈ In a small mixing bowl, combine the eggs, milk, and the melted butter and chocolate mixture. Add all at once to the flour mixture together with the raspberries. Stir until just moistened (the batter should be lumpy).

◈ Spoon batter into prepared muffin cups, filling them two-thirds full. Bake until golden brown and a wooden skewer or toothpick inserted into the center of a muffin comes out clean, 15–20 minutes. Remove from oven and cool in pan for 5 minutes. Serve warm, dusted with sifted confectioners' sugar.

spiced carrot and walnut muffins

makes 6 large muffins

¼ cup (2 oz/60 g) butter, chopped

1 tablespoon light molasses (golden syrup)

2¼ cups (11 oz/340 g) self-rising flour

2 teaspoons mixed spice

½ teaspoon baking soda
(bicarbonate of soda)

½ cup (3 oz/90 g) firmly packed dark
brown sugar

1 cup (5 oz/155 g) grated carrot
(1 medium carrot)

⅓ cup (1¼ oz/40 g) chopped walnuts

1 cup (8 fl oz/250 ml) milk

½ cup (4 fl oz/125 ml) light sour cream

2 eggs, lightly beaten

CREAM CHEESE FROSTING

3 oz (90 g) cream cheese, at room
temperature

1 oz (30 g) butter

1 teaspoon vanilla extract (essence)

1½ cups (7 oz/225 g) confectioners'
(icing) sugar, sifted

✥ Preheat oven to 400°F (200°C/Gas Mark 5). Grease six large (1-cup) muffin cups or line them with parchment (baking) paper cases.

✥ In a small saucepan over low heat, melt the butter and light molasses. Set aside to cool.

✥ In a large mixing bowl, sift together the flour, mixed spice, and baking soda. Stir through the brown sugar, carrot, and walnuts. Make a well in the center.

✥ In a small mixing bowl, combine the milk, sour cream, eggs, and the butter and light molasses mixture. Add all at once to the flour mixture and stir until just moistened (the batter should be lumpy).

✥ Spoon batter into prepared muffin cups, filling them two-thirds full. Bake until golden brown and a wooden skewer or toothpick inserted into the center of a muffin comes out clean, 25–30 minutes. Cool in pan for 5 minutes, then transfer to a wire rack. Allow to cool completely before icing.

✥ For frosting, using an electric mixer on medium to high speed, beat together the cream cheese, butter, and vanilla extract until light and fluffy. Gradually add the confectioners' sugar, beating until creamy and smooth. Spread over the cooled muffins.

lemon coconut muffins
with coconut topping

makes 12 standard muffins

2 cups (10 oz/315 g) self-rising flour

1 cup (3 oz/90 g) grated dried (desiccated) coconut

½ cup (4 oz/125 g) sugar

2 eggs, lightly beaten

1 cup (8 fl oz/250 ml) milk

⅓ cup (3 oz/90 g) butter, melted

2 teaspoons finely grated lemon zest

¼ cup (2 fl oz/60 ml) lemon juice

COCONUT STREUSEL TOPPING

½ cup (2½ oz/75 g) all-purpose (plain) flour

¼ cup (2 oz/60 g) sugar

¼ cup (¾ oz/25 g) grated dried (desiccated) coconut

¼ cup (2 oz/60 g) cold butter, cubed

❖ Preheat oven to 400°F (200°C/Gas Mark 5). Grease twelve standard (½-cup) muffin cups or line them with parchment (baking) paper cases.

❖ In a large mixing bowl, sift the self-rising flour. Stir through the coconut and sugar. Make a well in the center.

❖ In a small mixing bowl, combine the eggs, milk, butter, lemon zest, and juice. Add all at once to the flour mixture and stir until just moistened (the batter should be lumpy).

❖ Spoon batter into prepared muffin cups, filling them two-thirds full.

❖ For the coconut topping, place the flour, sugar, and coconut in a small bowl. Add the butter and rub in with your fingertips until the mixture resembles coarse crumbs. Spoon the topping evenly over the muffins.

❖ Bake until golden brown and a wooden skewer or toothpick inserted into the center of a muffin comes out clean, 15–20 minutes. Remove from oven and cool in pan for 5 minutes. Serve warm, or transfer to a wire rack to cool.

raspberry and almond muffins

Ground almonds give these muffins added moisture and an extra dimension of flavor. If using frozen raspberries, there is no need to thaw them first. If you can't find coffee crystals, any kind of coarse sugar can be substituted.

2 cups (10 oz/315 g) self-rising flour

⅔ cup (5½ oz/160 g) granulated (white) sugar

½ cup (3 oz/90 g) ground almonds

2 eggs, lightly beaten

1 cup (8 fl oz/250 ml) milk

¼ cup (2 oz/60 g) butter, melted

1 teaspoon vanilla extract (essence)

1½ cups (6 oz/185 g) fresh or frozen raspberries

½ cup (1½ oz/45 g) sliced (flaked) almonds

2 tablespoons coffee crystals (coffee sugar) or coarse sugar

✧ Preheat oven to 400°F (200°C/Gas Mark 5). Grease twelve standard (½-cup) muffin cups or line them with parchment (baking) paper cases.

✧ In a large mixing bowl, sift the flour. Stir through the sugar and almonds. Make a well in the center.

✧ In a small mixing bowl, combine the eggs, milk, butter, and vanilla. Add all at once to the flour mixture together with the raspberries and stir until just moistened (the batter should be lumpy).

✧ Spoon batter into prepared muffin cups, filling them two-thirds full. Sprinkle evenly with the sliced almonds and coffee crystals.

✧ Bake until golden brown and a wooden skewer or toothpick inserted into the center of a muffin comes out clean, 15–20 minutes. Remove from oven and cool in pan for 5 minutes. Serve warm, or transfer to a wire rack to cool.

food fact

Raspberries grow on low, thorny shrubs and have been cultivated for thousands of years. Red berries are the most common, but white, yellow, golden, and black varieties are also available. Raspberries are delicate and perishable, so check their condition before buying. Damp stains on the bottom of the carton indicate that some of the berries have deteriorated. Raspberries in good condition will keep for up to 2 days in the refrigerator. Wash only if necessary and always at the last minute. Frozen raspberries have a good flavor and texture and are especially suited to baking.

rolled oat, banana, and golden raisin muffins

makes 6 large muffins

Packed full of flavor and goodness, these are a great breakfast muffin. Use very ripe bananas, with skins well splotched with black, as they will be softer and sweeter. Mash them with a fork, adding a few drops of lemon juice, if you wish, to prevent the fruit from browning.

2 cups (10 oz/300 g) self-rising flour

1 teaspoon ground cinnamon

½ teaspoon baking soda (bicarbonate of soda)

1 cup (3½ oz/100 g) rolled oats

½ cup (2 oz/60 g) golden raisins (sultanas)

½ cup (3½ oz/105 g) firmly packed brown sugar

2 eggs, lightly beaten

¾ cup (6 fl oz/185 ml) milk

¼ cup (2 fl oz/60 ml) vegetable oil

2 medium mashed bananas, to yield about 1 cup (8 oz/250 g)

½ cup (3½ oz/105 g) demerara sugar

⅓ cup (1¼ oz/35 g) rolled oats, extra

◈ Preheat oven to 400°F (200°C/Gas Mark 5). Grease six large (1-cup) muffin cups or line them with parchment (baking) paper cases.

◈ In a large mixing bowl, sift together the flour, cinnamon, and baking soda. Stir through the rolled oats, golden raisins, and brown sugar. Make a well in the center.

◈ In a small mixing bowl, combine the eggs, milk, oil, and banana. Add all at once to the flour mixture and stir until just moistened (the batter should be lumpy).

◈ Spoon batter into prepared muffin cups, filling them two-thirds full. Sprinkle with the demerara sugar and the extra rolled oats.

◈ Bake until golden brown and a wooden skewer or toothpick inserted into the center of a muffin comes out clean, 25–30 minutes. Remove from oven and cool in pan for 5 minutes. Serve warm, or transfer to a wire rack to cool.

pear and raisin muffins

makes 12 standard muffins

These muffins are high in flavor but low in fat, making them an indulgent treat for those watching their fat intake. Use a pear that is ripe but firm for this recipe, so that the pieces will hold their shape when baked.

2 cups (10 oz/300 g) self-rising flour

1 teaspoon nutmeg

1/2 cup (3 oz/90 g) brown sugar

1/2 cup (2 oz/60 g) chopped raisins

2 eggs, lightly beaten

1 cup (8 fl oz/250 ml) pear or apple juice

1/3 cup (2¾ fl oz/80 ml) vegetable oil

1 large pear, peeled, cored and finely chopped

1/2 cup (2 oz/60 g) chopped walnuts

1/2 cup (3½ oz/110 g) raw sugar

✧ Preheat oven to 400°F (200°C/Gas Mark 5). Grease twelve standard (½-cup) muffin cups or line them with parchment (baking) paper cases.

✧ In a large mixing bowl, sift together the flour and nutmeg. Stir through the brown sugar and raisins. Make a well in the center.

✧ In a small mixing bowl, combine the eggs, juice, and oil. Add all at once to the flour mixture together with the chopped pear and stir until just moistened (the batter should be lumpy).

✧ Spoon batter into prepared muffin cups, filling them two-thirds full. Sprinkle with the walnuts and raw sugar.

✧ Bake until golden brown and a wooden skewer or toothpick inserted into the center of a muffin comes out clean, 15–20 minutes. Remove from oven and cool in pan for 5 minutes. Serve warm, or transfer to a wire rack to cool.

carrot, bran, and prune muffins

makes 6 large muffins

Soaking the bran in the milk makes these muffins extra moist. Dried or drained canned prunes can be used. Combined with carrot and bran, they give these muffins a healthful measure of fiber.

1 cup (2¼ oz/70 g) All-Bran cereal

1 cup (8 fl oz/250 ml) low-fat milk

2 cups (10 oz/300 g) all-purpose (plain) flour

1 tablespoon baking powder

1 teaspoon ground nutmeg

½ cup (3 oz/90 g) dark brown sugar

1 cup (5 oz/155 g) grated carrot (1 medium carrot)

½ cup (4 oz/125 g) chopped pitted prunes

2 eggs, lightly beaten

½ cup (4 fl oz/125 ml) light sour cream

⅓ cup (2¾ fl oz/80 ml) vegetable oil

◈ Preheat oven to 400°F (200°C/Gas Mark 5). Grease six large (1-cup) muffin cups or line them with parchment (baking) paper cases.

◈ In a small bowl, soak the All-Bran in the milk for 10 minutes to soften a little.

◈ In a large mixing bowl, sift together the flour, baking powder, and nutmeg. Stir through the brown sugar, grated carrot, and raisins. Make a well in the center.

◈ In a small mixing bowl, combine the eggs, sour cream, oil, and the bran and milk mixture. Add all at once to the flour mixture and stir until just moistened (the batter should be lumpy).

◈ Spoon batter into prepared muffin cups, filling them two-thirds full.

◈ Bake until golden brown and a wooden skewer or toothpick inserted into the center of a muffin comes out clean, 25–30 minutes. Remove from oven and cool in pan for 5 minutes. Serve warm, or transfer to a wire rack to cool.

savory *muffins*

cheesy buttermilk muffins

makes 12 standard muffins

2 cups (10 oz/315 g)
self-rising flour

1/2 teaspoon baking powder

1 cup (4 oz/125 g)
shredded Cheddar cheese

1/2 cup (1¾ oz/50 g)
grated Parmesan cheese

2 tablespoons
finely chopped parsley

1 egg, lightly beaten

1¼ cups (10 fl oz/315 ml)
buttermilk

⅓ cup (3 oz/90 g) butter,
melted

3 oz (90 g) marinated
feta cheese, crumbled

✥ Preheat oven to 400°F (200°C/Gas Mark 5). Grease twelve standard (½-cup) muffin cups or line them with parchment (baking) paper cases.

✥ In a large mixing bowl, sift together the flour and baking powder. Stir through the Cheddar cheese, Parmesan, and parsley. Make a well in the center.

✥ In a small mixing bowl, combine the egg, buttermilk, and butter. Add all at once to the flour mixture together with the crumbled feta. Stir until just moistened (the batter should be lumpy).

✥ Spoon batter into prepared muffin cups, filling them two-thirds full. Bake until golden brown and a wooden skewer or toothpick inserted into the center of a muffin comes out clean, 15–20 minutes. Cool in pan for 5 minutes. Serve warm, or transfer to a wire rack to cool.

ham and cheese rye muffins

makes 12 standard muffins

These muffins make a meal when served with a green salad or a bowl of soup. Any leftover muffins may be frozen, then reheated to serve later.

1¼ cups (6½ oz/190 g) all-purpose (plain) flour

⅓ cup (1¼ oz/35 g) rye flour

2 teaspoons baking powder

2 teaspoons sugar

¼ teaspoon caraway seed

¼ teaspoon onion salt

1 egg, lightly beaten

¾ cup (6 fl oz/185 ml) milk

¼ cup (2 fl oz/60 ml) vegetable oil

⅔ cup (3 oz/90 g) finely chopped fully cooked ham

1¼ cups (5 oz/155 g) shredded Swiss or Gruyère cheese

❖ Preheat oven to 400°F (200°C/Gas Mark 5). Lightly grease twelve standard (½-cup) muffin tins or line them with parchment (baking) paper cases.

❖ In a medium mixing bowl, stir together the flours, baking powder, sugar, caraway seed, and onion salt. Make a well in the center.

❖ In a small mixing bowl, combine the egg, milk, and oil. Add all at once to flour mixture together with the ham and 3 oz (90 g) of the cheese. Stir until just moistened (the batter should be lumpy).

❖ Spoon batter into prepared muffin cups, filling them two-thirds full. Bake until golden brown and a wooden skewer or toothpick inserted into the center of a muffin comes out clean, about 20 minutes. Sprinkle with the remaining 2 oz (60 g) cheese. Bake until cheese is melted, about 1 minute more.

❖ Remove from oven and cool in pan for 5 minutes. Serve warm, or transfer to a wire rack to cool.

food fact

Rye is a soft-textured, slightly sour grain that was formerly the staple in northern Europe due to its ability to tolerate colder conditions than wheat. Rye flour is slightly bitter and tangy, and makes a dense, heavy bread that keeps better than wheat bread. There are two types: dark rye flour, which retains more of the bran, and medium rye. Rye flour has some of the gluten-forming proteins that give bread its characteristic chewy texture, but fewer than wheat flour. If you wish, replace up to one third of a recipe's wheat flour with rye flour.

carrot and zucchini muffins

makes 12 standard muffins

Buttermilk imparts a
pleasant tang to these
muffins, and also reacts
with the baking powder
to help leaven them.

2 cups (10 oz/315 g) self-rising flour

1 teaspoon baking powder

1/2 cup (2 3/4 oz/80 g) grated carrot (1 small carrot)

1/2 cup (2 1/4 oz/70 g) grated zucchini (courgette)
(1 medium zucchini)

1/3 cup (1 1/4 oz/40 g) chopped walnuts

2 tablespoons chopped parsley

2 eggs, lightly beaten

1 1/4 cups (10 fl oz/315 ml) buttermilk

1/2 cup (2 oz/60 g) butter, melted

2 tablespoons sunflower seeds

◈ Preheat oven to 400°F (200°C/Gas Mark 5). Grease twelve standard (½-cup) muffin tins or line them with parchment (baking) paper cases.

◈ In a large mixing bowl, sift together the flour and baking powder. Stir through the carrot, zucchini, walnuts, and parsley. Make a well in the center.

◈ In a small mixing bowl, combine the eggs, buttermilk, and butter. Add all at once to the flour mixture and stir until just moistened (the batter should be lumpy).

◈ Spoon batter into prepared muffin cups, filling them two-thirds full. Sprinkle with the sunflower seeds.

◈ Bake until golden brown and a wooden skewer or toothpick inserted into the center of a muffin comes out clean, 15–20 minutes. Cool in pan for 5 minutes. Serve warm, or transfer to a wire rack to cool.

recipe variations

The sunflower seeds may be replaced with sesame or poppy seeds. If you wish, roast the sesame seeds for added flavor and crunch. Scatter an even layer of seeds on a baking sheet and place in a moderate oven until golden and fragrant, about 5 minutes. Shake the pan from time to time to prevent them from burning.

microwave bacon and cheese muffins

makes 12 standard muffins

This recipe is designed for a 650-watt microwave oven. If your oven uses a different wattage, adjust the cooking times accordingly. Test for doneness a minute or two before the end of the stated cooking time; if necessary, return the muffins to the oven for a little longer.

1 cup (5 oz/155 g) self-rising flour

1 tablespoon sugar

1 1/2 teaspoons baking powder

1/2 teaspoon paprika

1/2 cup (2 oz/60 g) shredded Cheddar cheese

2 slices (rashers) bacon, chopped and cooked until crisp

1/4 green bell pepper (capsicum), finely chopped

3 green (spring) onions, chopped

1/2 cup (125 ml/4 fl oz) milk

1/3 cup (3 fl oz/90 ml) vegetable oil

1 egg

◈ Place all ingredients in a large mixing bowl. Using a wooden spoon, mix together quickly until mixture is well combined.

◈ Spoon batter into 12 standard (½-cup) microwave-safe muffin cups. Elevate cups from the oven floor, arranging them six at a time around the outside of the turntable. Cook on high (100%) until well risen and spongy to the touch, 2½–3 minutes.

◈ When cooked, remove from oven and let stand in the cups for 5 minutes, loosely covered. Serve warm with butter, or transfer to a wire rack to cool.

◈ Cook the remaining batter in the same way.

recipe hint

Many muffin recipes cook well in the microwave oven, but as a general rule the best results are obtained from quickly mixed batters that contain liquid shortening (oil or melted butter). Traditional batters based on a creamed butter-and-sugar mixture fare less well. The addition of moisture-retaining ingredients such as grated vegetables or fruits, or the use of oil rather than butter, also produces good results. Always test for doneness with a wooden skewer or toothpick rather than relying on the way the muffins look; cooked muffins may still appear moist on top due to the lack of dry heat in the microwave oven.

corn, chile, and red bell pepper muffins

makes 12 standard muffins

Fresh corn kernels cut straight from the cob will give these muffins the best flavor, but drained canned or thawed frozen kernels may also be used. Increase the amount of chile if you prefer a hotter taste.

cornmeal (polenta), for sprinkling

2 cups (10 oz/315 g) self-rising flour

1 teaspoon baking powder

1 cup (5 oz/155 g) fine cornmeal (polenta)

1 cup (6½ oz/200 g) corn kernels

½ small red bell pepper (capsicum), finely chopped

½ small red chile, seeded and finely chopped

2 tablespoons finely chopped Italian (flatleaf) parsley

2 eggs, lightly beaten

1 cup (8 fl oz/250 ml) buttermilk

½ cup (4 oz/125 g) creamed corn

¼ cup (2 fl oz/60 ml) vegetable oil

✧ Preheat oven to 400°F (200°C/Gas Mark 5). Grease twelve standard (½-cup) muffin cups, then lightly sprinkle cups with cornmeal, tilting pan to distribute evenly. Tip out any excess.

✧ In a large mixing bowl, sift together the flour and baking powder. Stir through the 1 cup (5 oz/155 g) cornmeal, the corn kernels, bell pepper, chile, and parsley. Make a well in the center.

✧ In a small mixing bowl, combine the eggs, buttermilk, creamed corn, and oil. Add all at once to the flour mixture and stir until just moistened (the batter should be lumpy).

✧ Spoon batter into prepared muffin cups, filling them two-thirds full. Sprinkle tops with a little more cornmeal. Bake until golden brown and a wooden skewer or toothpick inserted into the center of a muffin comes out clean, 15–20 minutes. Remove from oven and cool in pan for 5 minutes. Serve warm, or transfer to a wire rack to cool.

zucchini, mint, and buttermilk muffins

makes 12 standard muffins

If fresh mint is not available, substitute another fresh herb, such as basil, cilantro (coriander), or parsley. Dried mint is unsuitable, as it lacks the zing of the fresh herb.

2 cups (10 oz/315 g) self-rising flour

½ teaspoon baking powder

2 tablespoons chopped fresh mint

2 eggs, lightly beaten

1 cup (8 fl oz/250 ml) buttermilk

3 oz (90 g) butter, melted

2 medium zucchini (courgettes), grated

2 tablespoons sunflower seeds

◈ Preheat oven to 400°F (200°C/Gas Mark 5). Grease twelve standard (½-cup) muffin cups or line them with parchment (baking) paper cases.

◈ In a large mixing bowl, sift together the flour and baking powder. Stir through the chopped mint. Make a well in the center.

◈ In a small mixing bowl, combine the eggs, buttermilk, butter, and grated zucchini. Add all at once to the flour mixture and stir until just moistened (the batter should be lumpy).

◈ Spoon batter into prepared muffin cups, filling them two-thirds full. Sprinkle with the sunflower seeds. Bake until golden brown and a wooden skewer or toothpick inserted into the center of a muffin comes out clean, 15–20 minutes. Cool in pan for 5 minutes. Serve warm, or transfer to a wire rack to cool.

food fact

Mint is a perennial herb with a bullying growing habit; if left unchecked, it will happily engulf its neighbors. There are some 25 species, which cross readily, even in the wild, resulting in a wide range of hybrids. The various types have different flavors, and some are highly scented, too. Spearmint is the variety most widely cultivated for culinary use; when a recipe calls simply for "mint," spearmint is usually implied. Fresh mint can be wrapped in damp paper towels and stored in a plastic bag in the refrigerator for up to 5 days. Just before using, rinse it well, as it can be sandy. Dry on paper towels before chopping.

corn, bacon, and thyme muffins

makes 12 standard muffins

This recipe uses soy milk, making it suitable for those who are lactose-intolerant. If you prefer, cows' milk can be used instead.

¾ oz (20 g) butter

3 slices (rashers) bacon, rind removed, finely chopped

3 green (spring) onions, finely chopped

2 cups (10 oz/315 g) self-rising flour

½ teaspoon baking powder

1 cup (6½ oz/200 g) corn kernels

1 tablespoon fresh thyme leaves

1 egg, lightly beaten

1½ cups (12 fl oz/375 ml) soy milk

3 oz (90 g) butter, extra, melted

12 small thyme sprigs

⟡ Preheat oven to 400°F (200°C/Gas Mark 5). Grease twelve standard (½-cup) muffin cups or line them with parchment (baking) paper cases.

⟡ In a small frying pan over medium heat, melt the butter. Add the bacon and green onions and cook, stirring, until the bacon is well cooked and the onions are soft, about 5 minutes. Set aside to cool.

⟡ In a large mixing bowl, sift together the flour and baking powder. Stir through the corn kernels and thyme leaves. Make a well in the center.

⟡ In a small mixing bowl, combine the beaten egg, soy milk, and the extra melted butter. Add all at once to the flour mixture together with the bacon and onion mixture. Stir until just moistened (the batter should be lumpy).

⟡ Spoon batter into prepared muffin cups, filling them two-thirds full. Place a thyme sprig on top of each muffin, pushing it a little into the batter.

⟡ Bake until golden brown and a wooden skewer or toothpick inserted into the center of a muffin comes out clean, 15–20 minutes. Cool in pan for 5 minutes. Serve warm, or transfer to a wire rack to cool.

onion, chile, and cheese muffins

makes 12 standard muffins

You can use any mixture
of herbs in this recipe:
try oregano, parsley,
marjoram, or basil.

¾ oz (20 g) butter

1 small red (Spanish) onion, finely chopped

1 red chile, seeded and finely chopped

2 cups (10 oz/315 g) self-rising flour

½ teaspoon baking powder

1 cup (4½ oz/130 g) shredded Gruyère cheese

3 tablespoons chopped mixed fresh herbs

2 eggs, lightly beaten

1 cup (8 fl oz/250 ml) milk

¼ cup (2 oz/60 g) butter, extra, melted

◈ Preheat oven to 400°F (200°C/Gas Mark 5). Grease twelve standard (½-cup) muffin cups or line them with parchment (baking) paper cases.

◈ In a small frying pan over medium heat, melt the butter. Add the onion and chile and cook, stirring, until softened but not browned, about 5 minutes. Set aside to cool.

◈ In a large mixing bowl, sift together the flour and baking powder. Stir through the shredded cheese and herbs. Make a well in the center.

◈ In a small mixing bowl, combine the beaten eggs, milk, and melted butter. Add all at once to the flour mixture together with the onion and chile mixture. Stir until just moistened (the batter should be lumpy).

◈ Spoon batter into prepared muffin cups, filling them two-thirds full. Bake until golden brown and a wooden skewer or toothpick inserted into the center of a muffin comes out clean, 15–20 minutes. Remove from oven and cool in pan for 5 minutes. Serve warm, or transfer to a wire rack to cool.

makes 10 standard muffins

1 cup (5 oz/155 g)
all-purpose flour

¾ cup (4½ oz/130 g)
whole wheat (wholemeal)
flour

1 tablespoon sugar

2 teaspoons baking powder

¼ teaspoon baking soda
(bicarbonate of soda)

¼ teaspoon salt

1 egg, beaten

¾ cup (6 fl oz/185 ml) milk

½ cup (5 oz/155 g) peeled
and finely grated carrot

¼ cup (2 fl oz/60 ml)
vegetable oil

2 tablespoons bought pesto

2 tablespoons grated
Parmesan cheese

❖ Preheat oven to 400°F (200°C/Gas Mark 5). Grease ten standard (½-cup) muffin cups or line them with parchment (baking) paper cases.

❖ In a large mixing bowl, sift together the flours, sugar, baking powder, baking soda, and salt. Make a well in the center.

❖ In a small bowl, combine egg, milk, carrot, and oil. Add all at once to the flour mixture and stir until just moistened (the batter should be lumpy).

❖ Spoon 1 heaping tablespoon of batter into each prepared muffin cup. Top with about 2 teaspoons of pesto, then with remaining batter, filling muffin cups two-thirds full. Sprinkle each muffin with about 2 teaspoons of Parmesan cheese.

❖ Bake until golden brown and a wooden skewer or toothpick inserted into the center of a muffin comes out clean, about 20 minutes. Remove from oven and cool in pan for 5 minutes. Serve warm, or transfer to a wire rack to cool.

carrot muffins
with pesto

mushroom and bacon muffins

makes 12 standard muffins

1/4 cup (2 fl oz/60 ml) olive oil

2 green (spring) onions,
finely chopped

2 slices (rashers) bacon,
rind removed, diced

3 oz (90 g) Swiss brown
mushrooms, finely chopped

2 cups (10 oz/315 g)
self-rising flour

1/2 teaspoon baking powder

2 eggs, lightly beaten

1 1/4 cups (10 fl oz/315 ml) milk

6 Swiss brown
mushrooms, sliced,
extra

❖ Preheat oven to 400°F (200°C/Gas Mark 5). Grease twelve standard (1/2-cup) muffin cups or line them with parchment (baking) paper cases.

❖ In a medium frying pan over medium heat, warm the oil. Add the spring onions, bacon, and mushrooms and cook, stirring, until softened, about 5 minutes. Set aside to cool.

❖ In a large mixing bowl, sift together the flour and baking powder. Make a well in the center.

❖ In a small mixing bowl, combine the eggs and milk. Add all at once to the flour mixture together with the mushroom mixture. Stir until just moistened (the batter should be lumpy).

❖ Spoon batter into prepared muffin cups, filling them two-thirds full. Divide the sliced extra mushrooms evenly over the top of the batter. Bake until golden brown and cooked through, 15–20 minutes. Cool in pan for 5 minutes. Serve warm, or transfer to a wire rack to cool.

smoked salmon and dill muffins

makes 12 standard muffins

2 cups (10 oz/315 g) self-rising flour

½ teaspoon baking powder

2 eggs, lightly beaten

½ cup (4 fl oz/125 ml) sour cream

½ cup (4 fl oz/125 ml) milk

⅓ cup (3 oz/90 g) butter, melted

1 tablespoon horseradish cream

4 oz (125 g) smoked salmon, chopped

2 tablespoons chopped fresh dill

❖ Preheat oven to 400°F (200°C/Gas Mark 5). Grease twelve standard (½-cup) muffin cups or line them with parchment (baking) paper cases.

❖ In a large mixing bowl, sift together the flour and baking powder. Make a well in the center.

❖ In a small mixing bowl, combine the eggs, sour cream, milk, butter, and horseradish cream. Add all at once to the flour mixture together with the smoked salmon and dill. Stir until just moistened (the batter should be lumpy).

❖ Spoon batter into prepared muffin cups, filling them two-thirds full. Bake until golden brown and cooked through, 15–20 minutes. Cool in pan for 5 minutes. Serve warm, or transfer to a wire rack to cool.

cornbread
mini muffins
with cheese and chives

makes 24 mini muffins

2 cups (10 oz/315 g)
self-rising flour

½ teaspoon baking powder

1 cup (5 oz/155 g) cornmeal
(polenta)

½ cup (2 oz/60 g) shredded
Cheddar cheese

½ cup (1¾ oz/50 g) grated
Parmesan cheese

2 tablespoons chopped chives

2 eggs, lightly beaten

1⅓ cups (11 fl oz/350 ml) milk

2 oz (60 g) butter, melted

⅓ cup (1¼ oz/35 g) grated
Parmesan cheese, extra

¼ cup cornmeal (polenta), extra

❖ Preheat oven to 400°F (200°C/Gas Mark 5).
Grease twenty-four mini muffin cups or line
them with parchment (baking) paper.

❖ In a large mixing bowl, sift together the flour
and baking powder. Stir through the cornmeal,
cheeses, and chives. Make a well in the center.

❖ In a small mixing bowl, combine the eggs,
milk, and butter. Add all at once to the flour
mixture and stir until just moistened (the batter
should be lumpy).

❖ Spoon batter into prepared muffin cups,
filling them two-thirds full. Sprinkle with extra
Parmesan and cornmeal. Bake until golden
brown and cooked through, 12–15 minutes.
Cool in pan for 5 minutes. Serve warm, or
transfer to a wire rack to cool.

131

pizza muffins

makes 12 standard muffins

1 tablespoon olive oil

¼ onion, finely chopped

*¼ red bell pepper
(capsicum), finely chopped*

1 clove garlic, crushed

*2 oz (60 g) fully cooked ham,
finely chopped*

*1 small tomato, peeled,
seeded, and chopped*

*2 cups (10 oz/315 g)
self-rising flour*

1 teaspoon baking powder

*½ cup (1¾ oz/50 g)
grated Parmesan cheese*

*1 tablespoon chopped
black olives*

*½ teaspoon dried oregano
leaves*

2 eggs, lightly beaten

1 cup (8 fl oz/250 ml) milk

*¼ cup (2 fl oz/60 ml)
olive oil, extra*

❖ Preheat oven to 400°F (200°C/Gas Mark 5). Grease twelve standard (½-cup) muffin cups or line them with parchment (baking) paper cases.

❖ In a medium frying pan over medium heat, warm the oil. Add the onion, bell pepper, and garlic and cook, stirring, until softened, about 5 minutes. Stir through the ham and tomato. Set aside to cool.

❖ In a large mixing bowl, sift together the flour and baking powder. Stir through the Parmesan, olives, and oregano. Make a well in the center.

❖ In a small mixing bowl, combine the egg, milk, and extra oil. Add all at once to the flour mixture together with the onion mixture. Stir until just moistened (the batter should be lumpy).

❖ Spoon batter into prepared muffin cups, filling them two-thirds full. Bake until golden brown and cooked through, 15–20 minutes. Cool in pan for 5 minutes. Serve warm, or transfer to a wire rack to cool.

fresh herb
whole wheat
muffins

makes 12 standard muffins

Serve these muffins instead
of bread with soup,
salad, or an omelet,
or spread with butter or
light cream cheese for
a healthful snack.

1 cup (5½ oz/170 g) whole wheat (wholemeal)
self-rising flour

1 cup (5 oz/155g) self-rising flour

½ teaspoon baking powder

2 tablespoons snipped fresh chives

2 tablespoons chopped fresh parsley

1 tablespoon chopped fresh mint

1 tablespoon chopped fresh oregano

2 eggs, lightly beaten

1¼ cups (10 fl oz/315 ml) plain yogurt

⅓ cup (3 oz/90 g) butter, melted

Preheat oven to 400°F (200°C/Gas Mark 5). Grease twelve standard (½-cup) muffin cups or line them with parchment (baking) paper cases.

In a large mixing bowl, sift together the flours and baking powder, returning the husks to the bowl. Stir through the chopped herbs. Make a well in the center.

In a small mixing bowl, combine the eggs, yogurt, and butter. Add all at once to the flour mixture and stir until just moistened (the batter should be lumpy).

Spoon batter into prepared muffin cups, filling them two-thirds full. Bake until golden brown and a wooden skewer or toothpick inserted into the center of a muffin comes out clean, 15–20 minutes. Remove from oven and cool in pan for 5 minutes. Serve warm, or transfer to a wire rack to cool.

recipe **hint**

Fresh herbs can be sandy, so rinse them well under running water or by swishing them gently in a bowl of cold water. To preserve their flavor and increase their storage life, do not wash them until just before use. Dry thoroughly on paper towels before chopping them, otherwise they will stick to the knife. As a rule, herbs are finely chopped, usually with a chef's knife. A pair of scissors or a mezzaluna (an Italian utensil with twin curved blades that are rocked back and forth over the food to be chopped) may also be used for mincing.

cornmeal, chile, and olive muffins

makes 6 large muffins

Where a recipe specifies cornmeal, yellow cornmeal (polenta) is usually implied, although white or blue cornmeal can also be used for these muffins. If you like a hotter flavor, increase the amount of chile. These muffins would make a good accompaniment for a Mexican meal.

2 cups (10 oz/315 g) self-rising flour

1 teaspoon baking powder

1 cup (5 oz/155 g) cornmeal (polenta)

1/3 cup (1 3/4 oz/50 g) chopped black olives

1/3 cup (1 3/4 oz/50 g) chopped green olives

1/2 small green chile, seeded and finely chopped

2 eggs, lightly beaten

1 1/4 cups (10 fl oz/315 ml) milk

1/3 cup (3 oz/90 g) butter, melted

1/2 cup (4 oz/125 g) creamed corn

1/3 cup (1 1/2 oz/40 g) pitted and sliced black olives

✧ Preheat oven to 400°F (200°C/Gas Mark 5). Grease six large (1-cup) muffin cups or line them with parchment (baking) paper cases.

✧ In a large mixing bowl, sift together the flour and baking powder. Stir through the cornmeal, black and green olives, and the chopped chile. Make a well in the center.

✧ In a small mixing bowl, combine the eggs, milk, butter, and creamed corn. Add all at once to the flour mixture and stir until just moistened (the batter should be lumpy).

✧ Spoon batter into prepared muffin cups, filling them two-thirds full. Top with the olive slices, pushing them a little into the batter.

✧ Bake until golden brown and a wooden skewer or toothpick inserted into the center of a muffin comes out clean, 25–30 minutes. Remove from oven and cool in pan for 5 minutes. Serve warm, or transfer to a wire rack to cool.

roasted red bell pepper and parsley
mini muffins

makes 24 mini muffins

If you're short of time, canned or bottled roasted bell peppers may be used in this recipe. The smoky flavor of the roasted bell peppers makes these muffins a good accompaniment for barbecued foods.

1 small red bell pepper (capsicum), quartered and seeded

oil, for brushing

2 cups (10 oz/315 g) self-rising flour

½ cup (1 oz/30 g) finely chopped parsley

2 eggs, lightly beaten

1¼ cups (10 fl oz/315 ml) buttermilk

2 oz (60 g) butter, melted

Preheat oven to 400°F (200°C/Gas Mark 5). Grease twenty-four mini-muffin cups.

Lightly brush the bell pepper with oil and place, skin side up, under a preheated broiler (grill). Broil (grill) until the skin is blackened and the flesh has softened. Cool, then peel. Finely chop the flesh.

In a large mixing bowl, sift the flour. Stir through the parsley. Make a well in the center.

In a small mixing bowl, combine the beaten eggs, buttermilk, and butter. Add all at once to the flour mixture together with the chopped bell pepper. Stir until just moistened (the batter should be lumpy).

Spoon batter into prepared muffin cups, filling them two-thirds full. Bake until golden brown and a wooden skewer or toothpick inserted into the center of a muffin comes out clean, 12–15 minutes. Remove from oven and cool in pan for 5 minutes. Serve warm, or transfer to a wire rack to cool.

recipe hint

Once roasted, put the hot bell peppers in a plastic bag, seal, and leave for 10 minutes. The steam created will loosen the skins, making the peppers easier to peel.

sun-dried tomato and camembert muffins

makes 12 standard muffins

Mediterranean flavors
of tomato, cheese, and
basil make these muffins
perfect for a summer
brunch or lunch.

2 cups (10 oz/315 g) self-rising flour

1/2 teaspoon baking powder

31/2 oz (100 g) drained, oil-packed, sun-dried tomatoes,
finely chopped

31/2 oz (100 g) Camembert cheese, finely chopped

2 tablespoons finely chopped fresh basil leaves

2 eggs, lightly beaten

1 cup (8 fl oz/250 ml) milk

1/3 cup (3 oz/90 g) butter, melted

❖ Preheat oven to 400°F (200°C/Gas Mark 5). Grease twelve standard (½-cup) muffin cups or line them with parchment (baking) paper cases.

❖ In a large mixing bowl, sift together the flour and baking powder. Stir through the sun-dried tomatoes, Camembert, and basil. Make a well in the center.

❖ In a small mixing bowl, combine the eggs, milk, and butter. Add all at once to the flour mixture and stir until just moistened (the batter should be lumpy).

❖ Spoon batter into prepared muffin cups, filling them two-thirds full. Bake until golden brown and a wooden skewer or toothpick inserted into the center of a muffin comes out clean, 15–20 minutes. Remove from oven and cool in pan for 5 minutes. Serve warm, or transfer to a wire rack to cool.

pumpkin, cheese, and oregano muffins

makes 6 large muffins

For use in cooking, choose small, sweet varieties of pumpkin with thick flesh and a small seed cavity, such as Sugar Pie, Baby Bear, or Cheese varieties. Butternut squash is also suitable.

10 oz (315 g) pumpkin, seeded, peeled, and cubed

2 cups (10 oz/315 g) self-rising flour

1 teaspoon baking powder

1 cup (4½ oz/130 g) grated fontina cheese

¼ cup (¾ oz/25 g) grated Parmesan cheese

2 tablespoons chopped fresh oregano

1 egg, lightly beaten

1 cup (8 fl oz/250 ml) milk

¼ cup (2 oz/60 g) butter, melted

2 tablespoons pumpkin seeds (pepitas)

- Preheat oven to 400°F (200°C/Gas Mark 5). Grease six large (1-cup) muffin cups or line them with parchment (baking) paper cases.

- Steam or microwave the pumpkin until tender when pierced with a fork. Cool, then mash.

- In a large mixing bowl, sift together the flour and baking powder. Stir through the grated fontina, Parmesan, and chopped oregano. Make a well in the center.

- In a small mixing bowl, combine the egg, milk, butter, and pumpkin. Add all at once to the flour mixture and stir until just moistened (the batter should be lumpy).

- Spoon batter into prepared muffin cups, filling them two-thirds full. Sprinkle with the pumpkin seeds.

- Bake until golden brown and a wooden skewer or toothpick inserted into the center of a muffin comes out clean, 25–30 minutes. Remove from oven and cool in pan for 5 minutes. Serve warm, or transfer to a wire rack to cool.

leek, parmesan, and ham muffins

makes 12 standard muffins

Leeks have a subtle oniony flavor that has an affinity with cheese. To prepare leeks, cut off most of the green top, then make two 2-inch (5-cm) deep cuts at right angles down through the stem. Plunge the leek vigorously up and down in a bowl or sink full of water to dislodge any trapped soil.

1 oz (30 g) butter

1 small leek, white part only, thinly sliced

2 cups (10 oz/315 g) self-rising flour

1/2 teaspoon baking powder

1/2 cup (1 3/4 oz/50 g) grated Parmesan cheese

3 oz (90 g) fully cooked ham, finely chopped

2 tablespoons chopped fresh sage leaves

1 egg, lightly beaten

1 1/4 cups (10 fl oz/315 ml) buttermilk

1/3 cup (3 oz/90 g) butter, melted

2 tablespoons sesame seeds

1/3 cup (1 1/4 oz/35 g) grated Parmesan cheese, extra

⬦ Preheat oven to 400°F (200°C/Gas Mark 5). Grease twelve standard (½-cup) muffin cups or line them with parchment (baking) paper cases.

⬦ In a small frying pan over medium heat, melt the butter. Add the leek and cook, stirring, until golden and softened but not browned, about 5 minutes. Set aside to cool.

⬦ In a large mixing bowl, sift together the flour and baking powder. Stir through the grated Parmesan, chopped ham, and sage leaves. Make a well in the center.

⬦ In a small mixing bowl, combine the egg, buttermilk, and butter. Add all at once to the flour mixture and stir until just moistened (the batter should be lumpy).

⬦ Spoon batter into prepared muffin cups, filling them two-thirds full. Sprinkle with the sesame seeds and the extra Parmesan.

⬦ Bake until golden brown and a wooden skewer or toothpick inserted into the center of a muffin comes out clean, 15–20 minutes. Remove from oven and cool in pan for 5 minutes. Serve warm, or transfer to a wire rack to cool.

pesto, pine nut, and parmesan muffins

makes 12 standard muffins

Pine nuts, the seeds of pine trees, are small and rich, with a soft texture and slightly piney flavor. They may be eaten raw, but are best lightly fried or roasted to intensify their flavor.

½ cup (2¾ oz/80 g) pine nuts

2 cups (10 oz/315 g) self-rising flour

½ teaspoon baking powder

1 cup (3½ oz/100 g) grated Parmesan cheese

2 tablespoons finely chopped fresh basil leaves

1 egg, lightly beaten

1 cup (8 fl oz/250 ml) milk

3 oz (90 g) butter, melted

¼ cup (2 oz/60 g) bought pesto

⅓ cup (1¼ oz/35 g) grated Parmesan, extra

◈ Preheat oven to 400°F (200°C/Gas Mark 5). Grease twelve standard (½-cup) muffin cups or line them with parchment (baking) paper cases.

◈ While the oven is heating, place the pine nuts on a baking sheet. Toast, checking frequently and shaking the baking sheet from time to time, until lightly golden, about 5 minutes. Watch them carefully, as they burn easily. Remove from oven and transfer to a small bowl so that they do not cook further due to the residual heat in the baking sheet. Allow to cool.

◈ In a large mixing bowl, sift together the flour and baking powder. Stir through the Parmesan, basil, and pine nuts. Make a well in the center.

◈ In a small mixing bowl, combine the egg, milk, butter, and pesto. Add all at once to the flour mixture and stir until just moistened (the batter should be lumpy).

◈ Spoon batter into prepared muffin cups, filling them two-thirds full. Sprinkle with the extra grated Parmesan.

◈ Bake until golden brown and a wooden skewer or toothpick inserted into the center of a muffin comes out clean, 15–20 minutes. Remove from oven and cool in pan for 5 minutes. Serve warm, or transfer to a wire rack to cool.

italian sausage and sage muffins

makes 12 standard muffins

Italian sausages are typically made of pork and may be spiced or mild. If they are unavailable, any well-flavored fresh sausage may be substituted.

1 tablespoon olive oil

4 oz (125 g) Italian sausages, well pricked

2 cups (10 oz/315 g) self-rising flour

1/2 teaspoon baking powder

2 eggs, lightly beaten

1 cup (8 fl oz/250 ml) milk

1/4 cup (2 fl oz/60 ml) olive oil, extra

2 tablespoons finely shredded fresh sage leaves

✥ Preheat oven to 400°F (200°C/Gas Mark 5). Grease twelve standard (½-cup) muffin cups or line them with parchment (baking) paper cases.

✥ In a medium frying pan over medium-high heat, warm the 1 tablespoon oil. Add the sausages and cook, turning to brown evenly, until cooked through, about 15 minutes. Remove from pan, drain on paper towels, and allow to cool. When cool, remove the outer casing and finely crumble the meat. Set aside.

✥ In a large mixing bowl, sift together the flour and baking powder. Make a well in the center.

✥ In a small mixing bowl, combine the beaten eggs, milk, and extra ¼ cup (2 fl oz/60 ml) oil. Add all at once to the flour mixture together with the crumbled sausage and sage. Stir until just moistened (the batter should be lumpy).

✥ Spoon batter into the prepared muffin cups, filling them two-thirds full.

✥ Bake until golden brown and a wooden skewer or toothpick inserted into the center of a muffin comes out clean, 15–20 minutes. Remove from oven and cool in pan for 5 minutes. Serve warm, or transfer to a wire rack to cool.

cheddar cheese
and herb muffins

You can use any mixture of
herbs for this recipe. Try
combining oregano, parsley,
marjoram, and thyme.

1 oz (30 g) butter

3 green (spring) onions, finely chopped

1 clove garlic, finely chopped

2 cups (10 oz/315 g) self-rising flour

1/2 teaspoon baking powder

1 cup (4 oz/125 g) shredded Cheddar cheese

1/2 cup (1 oz/30 g) finely chopped mixed fresh herbs

2 eggs, lightly beaten

1 1/4 cups (10 fl oz/315 ml) light sour cream

1/3 cup (3 oz/90 g) butter, melted

◈ Preheat oven to 400°F (200°C/Gas Mark 5). Grease twelve standard (½-cup) muffin cups or line them with parchment (baking) paper cases.

◈ In a small frying pan over medium heat, melt the butter. Add the green onion and garlic and cook until softened but not browned, 3–5 minutes. Set aside to cool.

◈ In a large mixing bowl, sift together the flour and baking powder. Stir through the Cheddar and herbs. Make a well in the center.

◈ In a small mixing bowl, combine the eggs, sour cream, and melted butter. Add all at once to the flour mixture together with the cooled onion and garlic mixture. Stir until just moistened (the batter should be lumpy).

◈ Spoon batter into prepared muffin cups, filling them two-thirds full.

◈ Bake until golden brown and a wooden skewer or toothpick inserted into the center of a muffin comes out clean, 15–20 minutes. Remove from oven and cool in pan for 5 minutes. Serve warm, or transfer to a wire rack to cool.

apple, onion, and thyme muffins

makes 12 standard muffins

The hearty flavor of these muffins echoes that of a traditional stuffing for roast chicken. Serve them with roast meat or a chicken dish.

1 oz (30 g) butter

1 small red (Spanish) onion, finely chopped

1/2 small red chile, seeded and finely chopped

2 cups (10 oz/315 g) self-rising flour

1/2 teaspoon baking powder

1 cup (4 oz/125 g) shredded Cheddar cheese

1 apple, peeled, cored, and finely chopped

2 tablespoons fresh thyme leaves

2 eggs, lightly beaten

1 cup (8 fl oz/250 ml) milk

1/4 cup (2 oz/60 g) butter, extra, melted

✧ Preheat oven to 400°F (200°C/Gas Mark 5). Grease twelve standard (½-cup) muffin cups or line them with parchment (baking) paper cases.

✧ In a small frying pan over medium heat, melt the butter. Add the onion and chile and cook, stirring, until softened but not browned, about 5 minutes. Set aside to cool.

✧ In a large mixing bowl, sift together the flour and baking powder. Stir through the cheese, apple, and thyme. Make a well in the center.

✧ In a small mixing bowl, combine the eggs, milk, and extra butter. Add all at once to the flour mixture together with the onion and chile mixture. Stir until just moistened (the batter should be lumpy).

✧ Spoon batter into prepared muffin cups, filling them two-thirds full.

✧ Bake until golden brown and a wooden skewer or toothpick inserted into the center of a muffin comes out clean, 15–20 minutes. Remove from oven and cool in pan for 5 minutes. Serve warm, or transfer to a wire rack to cool.

asparagus, cheese, and chive muffins

makes 12 standard muffins

Make these muffins in spring, when fresh asparagus is abundant and inexpensive. The flavor and texture of the fresh vegetable are totally unlike those of the canned variety. These muffins contain soy milk, making them suitable for those who are lactose intolerant.

6 thin stalks fresh asparagus

1½ cups (7 oz/225 g) self-rising flour

½ cup (3 oz/85 g) whole wheat (wholemeal) self-rising flour

½ teaspoon baking powder

½ cup (1¾ oz/50 g) grated Parmesan cheese

½ cup (2 oz/60 g) shredded Gouda cheese

2 tablespoons snipped chives

1 egg, lightly beaten

1½ cups (12 fl oz/375 ml) soy milk

¼ cup (2 fl oz/60 ml) vegetable oil

⅓ cup (1¼ oz/40 g) grated Parmesan cheese, extra

⅓ cup (1¼ oz/40 g) shredded Gouda cheese, extra

◈ Preheat oven to 400°F (200°C/Gas Mark 5). Grease twelve standard (½-cup) muffin cups or line them with parchment (baking) paper cases.

◈ Trim the tough ends from the asparagus and cut the stalks into ½-inch (1-cm) pieces. Steam or microwave until tender, 1½–3 minutes depending on the thickness of the spears. Cool.

◈ In a large mixing bowl, sift together the flours and baking powder, returning the husks to the bowl. Stir through the Parmesan, Gouda, and chives. Make a well in the center.

◈ In a small mixing bowl, combine the egg, soy milk, and oil. Add all at once to the flour mixture together with the cooled asparagus pieces. Stir until just moistened (the batter should be lumpy).

◈ Spoon batter into prepared muffin cups, filling them two-thirds full. Combine the extra Parmesan and Gouda cheeses and sprinkle evenly over the muffins.

◈ Bake until golden brown and a wooden skewer or toothpick inserted into the center of a muffin comes out clean, 15–20 minutes. Remove from oven and cool in pan for 5 minutes. Serve warm, or transfer to a wire rack to cool.

carrot, pineapple, and parsley muffins

makes 12 standard muffins

These savory-sweet muffins have a pleasing tang, and contain a healthful amount of fiber, too.

7 oz (225 g) can unsweetened pineapple slices or chunks, drained, juice reserved

1½ cups (7 oz/225 g) self-rising flour

½ cup (3 oz/85 g) whole wheat (wholemeal) self-rising flour

1 teaspoon baking powder

1 cup (3 oz/90 g) grated carrot (1 medium carrot)

3 tablespoons finely chopped fresh Italian (flatleaf) parsley

1 egg, lightly beaten

½ cup (4 fl oz/125 ml) milk

¼ cup (2 fl oz/60 ml) vegetable oil

✥ Preheat oven to 400°F (200°C/Gas Mark 5). Grease twelve standard (½-cup) muffin cups or line them with parchment (baking) paper cases.

✥ Crush the pineapple and its juice in a food processor. Set aside.

✥ In a large mixing bowl, sift together the flours and baking powder, returning the husks to the bowl. Stir through the grated carrot and parsley. Make a well in the center.

✥ In a small mixing bowl, combine the crushed pineapple, beaten egg, milk, and oil. Add all at once to the flour mixture together with the pineapple and juice. Stir just until moistened (the batter should be lumpy).

✥ Spoon batter into prepared muffin cups, filling them two-thirds full.

✥ Bake until golden brown and a wooden skewer or toothpick inserted into the center of a muffin comes out clean, 15–20 minutes. Remove from oven and cool in pan for 5 minutes. Serve warm, or transfer to a wire rack to cool.

semi-dried tomato, chile, and corn muffins

makes 12 standard muffins

Fresh corn kernels cut straight from the cob will give these muffins the best flavor, but drained canned or thawed frozen kernels may also be used. Increase the amount of chile if you prefer a hotter taste.

2 cups (10 oz/315 g) self-rising flour

½ teaspoon baking powder

1 cup (6½ oz/200 g) corn kernels

3 oz (90 g) semi-dried tomatoes, finely chopped

1 small green chile, seeded and finely chopped

1 egg, lightly beaten

¾ cup (6 fl oz/185 ml) milk

½ cup (4 fl oz/125 ml) light sour cream

¼ cup (2 fl oz/60 ml) vegetable oil

◈ Preheat oven to 400°F (200°C/Gas Mark 5). Grease twelve standard (½-cup) muffin cups or line them with parchment (baking) paper cases.

◈ In a large mixing bowl, sift together the flour and baking powder. Stir through the corn kernels, tomatoes, and chile. Make a well in the center.

◈ In a small mixing bowl, combine the egg, milk, sour cream, and oil. Add all at once to the flour mixture and stir until just moistened (the batter should be lumpy).

◈ Spoon batter into prepared muffin cups, filling them two-thirds full.

◈ Bake until golden brown and a wooden skewer or toothpick inserted into the center of a muffin comes out clean, 15–20 minutes. Remove from oven and cool in pan for 5 minutes. Serve warm, or transfer to a wire rack to cool.

recipe hint

Semi-dried tomatoes are easy to make at home, and a good way to use up a late-summer glut of the fruit.
1. Halve tomatoes lengthways and remove seeds. Salt lightly if desired.
2. Arrange slices, cut side down, directly on oven racks.
3. Set oven to 140°F (60°C/ Gas Mark ½). Place tomatoes in oven until slightly dried and shriveled but not leathery, 6–8 hours or overnight.
4. Store semi-dried tomatoes in an airtight container in the refrigerator for up to 1 week.

pumpkin and oat bran muffins

makes 6 large muffins

The warm spiciness of nutmeg complements pumpkin's natural sweetness. Use whole nutmeg in preference to ground, where possible. It gives the best flavor, as well as keeping its flavor much longer than the ground spice. Special nutmeg graters are available, or use the finest gauge of an ordinary grater.

10 oz (315 g) pumpkin, seeded, peeled, and cubed

2 cups (10 oz/315 g) all-purpose (plain) flour

1 tablespoon baking powder

1 teaspoon ground nutmeg

1 cup (5 oz/155 g) oat bran

2 eggs, lightly beaten

3/4 cup (6 fl oz/185 ml) milk

2 oz (60 g) butter, melted

✧ Preheat oven to 400°F (200°C/Gas Mark 5). Grease six large (1-cup) muffin cups. Line each with a 6-inch (15-cm) square of brown or parchment (baking) paper, roughly pleating to fit into the muffin cups, or line them with parchment (baking) paper cases.

✧ Steam or microwave the pumpkin until tender when pierced with a fork. Cool, then mash.

✧ In a large mixing bowl, sift together the flour, baking powder, and nutmeg. Stir through the oat bran. Make a well in the center.

✧ In a small mixing bowl, combine the eggs, milk, butter, and mashed pumpkin. Add all at once to the flour mixture and stir until just moistened (the batter should be lumpy).

✧ Spoon batter into prepared muffin cups, filling them two-thirds full.

✧ Bake until golden brown and a wooden skewer or toothpick inserted into the center of a muffin comes out clean, 25–30 minutes. Remove from oven and cool in pan for 5 minutes. Serve warm, or transfer to a wire rack to cool.

sun-dried bell pepper, olive, and onion muffins

makes 12 standard muffins

Use sun-dried tomatoes if the bell pepper (capsicum) is not available. If you wish, use marinated feta rather than plain; the herbs in the marinade will add extra flavor to the muffins.

2 tablespoons vegetable oil

1 red (Spanish) onion, thinly sliced

2 cups (10 oz/315 g) self-rising flour

½ teaspoon baking powder

2 eggs, lightly beaten

1 cup (8 fl oz/250 ml) low-fat milk

¼ cup (2 fl oz/60 ml) vegetable oil, extra

2 oz (60 g) feta cheese, crumbled

3 oz (90 g) sun-dried bell pepper (capsicum), finely chopped

½ cup (2½ oz/75 g) chopped black olives

◈ Preheat oven to 400°F (200°C/Gas Mark 5). Grease twelve standard (½-cup) muffin cups or line them with parchment (baking) paper cases.

◈ In a frying pan over medium heat, warm the 2 tablespoons oil. Add the onion and cook, stirring, until softened but not browned, about 10 minutes. Set aside to cool.

◈ In a large mixing bowl, sift together the flour and baking powder. Make a well in the center.

◈ In a small mixing bowl, combine the beaten egg, milk, and the extra ¼ cup (2 fl oz/60 ml) oil. Add all at once to the flour mixture together with the two-thirds of the onion, the crumbled feta, bell pepper, and olives. Stir until just moistened (the batter should be lumpy).

◈ Spoon batter into prepared muffin cups, filling them two-thirds full. Divide the remaining onion slices evenly over the top of the muffins.

◈ Bake until golden brown and a wooden skewer or toothpick inserted into the center of a muffin comes out clean, 15–20 minutes. Remove from oven and cool in pan for 5 minutes. Serve warm, or transfer to a wire rack to cool.

whole wheat, walnut, and pesto muffins

makes 12 standard muffins

Use a mild-flavored oil for these muffins, such as canola (rapeseed), corn, safflower, or sunflower seed oil, or a blended vegetable oil.

1 cup (5½ oz/170 g) whole wheat (wholemeal) self-rising flour

1 cup (5 oz/155 g) self-rising flour

½ teaspoon baking powder

½ cup (1¾ oz/50 g) grated Parmesan cheese

½ cup (2 oz/60 g) chopped walnuts

2 eggs, lightly beaten

1 cup (8 fl oz/250 ml) milk

¼ cup (2 fl oz/60 ml) vegetable oil (see note)

⅓ cup (3 oz/90 g) bought pesto

✧ Preheat oven to 400°F (200°C/Gas Mark 5). Grease twelve standard (½-cup) muffin cups or line them with parchment (baking) paper cases.

✧ In a large mixing bowl, sift the flours and baking powder, returning husks to the bowl. Stir through the Parmesan and walnuts. Make a well in the center.

✧ In a small mixing bowl, combine the eggs, milk, oil, and pesto. Add all at once to the flour mixture and stir until just moistened (the batter should be lumpy).

✧ Spoon batter into prepared muffin cups, filling them two-thirds full.

✧ Bake until golden brown and a wooden skewer or toothpick inserted into the center of a muffin comes out clean, 15–20 minutes. Remove from oven and cool in pan for 5 minutes. Serve warm, or transfer to a wire rack to cool.

zucchini, yogurt, and pecan muffins

makes 12 standard muffins

There is no need to peel the
zucchini for this recipe.
Simply wash, trim the ends,
then shred on the medium
gauge of a hand-held grater,
or use a food processor
fitted with a shredding disk.

2 cups (10 oz/315 g) self-rising flour

1/2 cup (2 oz/60 g) chopped pecans

3 tablespoons chopped fresh mint leaves

2 eggs, lightly beaten

1 1/4 cups (10 fl oz/315 ml) plain yogurt

1/3 cup (3 oz/90 g) butter, melted

1 cup (5 oz/155 g) shredded zucchini (courgette)
(2 medium zucchini)

12 pecan halves, extra

◈ Preheat oven to 400°F (200°C/Gas Mark 5). Grease twelve standard (½-cup) muffin cups or line them with parchment (baking) paper cases.

◈ In a large mixing bowl, sift the flour. Stir through the chopped pecans and chopped mint. Make a well in the center.

◈ In a small mixing bowl, combine eggs, yogurt, and butter. Add all at once to the flour mixture, together with the zucchini. Stir until just moistened (the batter should be lumpy).

◈ Spoon batter into prepared muffin cups, filling them two-thirds full. Place a pecan half on top of each muffin.

◈ Bake until golden brown and a wooden skewer or toothpick inserted into the center of a muffin comes out clean, 15–20 minutes. Remove from oven and cool in pan for 5 minutes. Serve warm, or transfer to a wire rack to cool.

makes 12 standard muffins

2 tablespoons (1 oz/30 g) butter

1 onion, thinly sliced

1 tablespoon firmly packed brown sugar

1 tablespoon balsamic vinegar

2 tablespoons fresh thyme leaves

2 cups (10 oz/315 g) self-rising flour

½ teaspoon baking powder.

2 eggs, lightly beaten

1 cup (8 fl oz/250 ml) milk

2 oz (60 g) butter, extra, melted

❖ Preheat oven to 400°F (200°C/Gas Mark 5). Grease twelve standard (½-cup) muffin cups or line them with parchment (baking) paper cases.

❖ In a small saucepan over low heat, melt the butter. Add the onion and cook, stirring, until softened but not browned, about 20 minutes. Add the brown sugar, balsamic, and thyme and cook over low heat for 5 minutes more. Set aside to cool.

❖ In a large mixing bowl, sift together the flour and baking powder. Make a well in the center.

❖ In a small mixing bowl, combine the eggs, milk, and extra butter. Add all at once to the flour mixture together with the onion mixture. Stir until just moistened (the batter should be lumpy).

❖ Spoon batter into prepared muffin cups, filling them two-thirds full. Bake until golden brown and cooked through, 15–20 minutes. Remove from oven and cool in pan for 5 minutes. Serve warm, or transfer to a wire rack to cool.

caramelized onion
and thyme muffins

ham, olive, and cheese
mini muffins

makes 24 mini muffins

*2 cups (10 oz/315 g)
self-rising flour*

*½ teaspoon baking
powder*

*1 cup (4 oz/125 g) finely
shredded Cheddar cheese*

*3 oz (90 g) ham,
finely chopped*

*½ cup (2½ oz/75 g)
finely chopped black
olives*

*2 tablespoons
snipped chives*

2 eggs, lightly beaten

*1 cup (8 fl oz/250 ml)
milk*

*2 oz (60 g) butter,
melted*

❖ Preheat oven to 400°F (200°C/Gas Mark 5). Grease twenty-four mini muffin cups or line them with parchment (baking) paper cases.

❖ In a large mixing bowl, sift together the flour and baking powder. Stir through the cheese, ham, olives, and chives. Make a well in the center.

❖ In a small mixing bowl, combine the eggs, milk, and butter. Add all at once to the flour mixture and stir until just moistened (the batter should be lumpy).

❖ Spoon batter into prepared muffin cups, filling them two-thirds full. Bake until golden brown, 12–15 minutes. Cool in pan for 5 minutes. Serve warm, or transfer to a wire rack to cool.

sweet potato, rosemary, and sesame muffins

makes 12 standard muffins

8 oz (250 g) sweet potato, peeled and cubed

2 cups (10 oz/315 g) self-rising flour

1 teaspoon baking powder

½ cup (2 oz/60 g) shredded Cheddar cheese

1 tablespoon chopped fresh rosemary

1 egg, lightly beaten

1 cup (8 fl oz/250 ml) buttermilk

¼ cup (2 oz/60 g) butter, melted

2 tablespoons sesame seeds, for sprinkling

❖ Preheat oven to 400°F (200°C/Gas Mark 5). Grease twelve standard (½-cup) muffin cups or line them with parchment (baking) paper cases.

❖ Steam or microwave the sweet potato until tender when pierced with a fork. Cool, then mash.

❖ In a large mixing bowl, sift together the flour and baking powder. Stir through the cheese and rosemary. Make a well in the center.

❖ In a small mixing bowl, combine the egg, buttermilk, butter, and sweet potato. Add all at once to the flour mixture and stir until just moistened (the batter should be lumpy).

❖ Spoon batter into prepared muffin cups, filling them two-thirds full. Sprinkle with the sesame seeds. Bake until golden brown and cooked through, 15–20 minutes. Cool in pan for 5 minutes. Serve warm, or transfer to a wire rack to cool.

174

spinach and feta muffins

makes 12 standard muffins

8 oz (250 g) packet frozen
chopped spinach, thawed

2 cups (10 oz/315 g)
self-rising flour

1 teaspoon baking powder

1 teaspoon ground nutmeg

2/3 cup (3 oz/90 g)
feta cheese, crumbled

1/2 cup (1¾ oz/50 g)
shredded Parmesan

2 eggs, lightly beaten

1 cup (8 fl oz/250 ml) milk

1/4 cup (2 oz/60 g)
butter, melted

❖ Preheat oven to 400°F (200°C/Gas Mark 5). Grease twelve standard (½-cup) muffin cups or line them with parchment (baking) paper cases.

❖ Use your hands to squeeze the excess moisture from the spinach.

❖ In a large mixing bowl, sift together the flour, baking powder, and nutmeg. Stir through the feta and Parmesan. Make a well in the center.

❖ In a small mixing bowl, combine the eggs, milk, butter, and spinach. Add all at once to the flour mixture and stir until just moistened (the batter should be lumpy).

❖ Spoon batter into prepared muffin cups, filling them two-thirds full. Bake until golden brown, 15–20 minutes. Cool in pan for 5 minutes. Serve warm, or transfer to a wire rack to cool.

sun-dried tomato, olive, and herb muffins

makes 12 standard muffins

*1½ cups (7 oz/225 g)
self-rising flour*

*1⅓ cups (7½ oz/230 g) whole
wheat (wholemeal)
self-rising flour*

*12 drained, oil-packed,
sun-dried tomatoes, sliced*

*⅔ cup (3 oz/90 g) black olives
(preferably Kalamata),
pitted and sliced*

*2 tablespoons chopped
fresh rosemary*

*⅓ cup (3 oz/90 g)
butter, melted*

1 egg, lightly beaten

*¾ cup (6 fl oz/185 ml)
light (single) cream*

½ cup (4 fl oz/125 ml) milk

*1⅔ cups (5½ oz/165 g)
grated Parmesan cheese*

*cream cheese, to serve
(optional)*

✤ Preheat oven to 400°F (200°C/Gas Mark 5). Grease twelve standard (½-cup) muffin cups or line them with parchment (baking) paper cases.

✤ In a large mixing bowl, sift together the flours, returning the husks to the bowl. Add the tomatoes, olives, and rosemary. Mix well.

✤ In medium mixing bowl, combine the butter, egg, cream, milk, and Parmesan cheese. Whisk until well combined. Add all at once to the flour mixture and stir until just moistened (the batter should be lumpy).

✤ Spoon batter into prepared muffin cups, filling them two-thirds full. Bake until golden brown and a wooden skewer or toothpick inserted into the center of a muffin comes out clean, about 25 minutes. Cool in pan for 5 minutes. Serve warm, or transfer to a wire rack to cool.

✤ To serve, cut each muffin in half and spread with cream cheese if desired.

avocado, cheddar, and bacon muffins

makes 12 standard muffins

Buttery, rich avocados pair well with bacon and cheese. The fruit should yield to gentle finger pressure when ripe. To ripen an unripe avocado, place it in a paper bag with an apple, a banana, or a tomato. Ethylene gases given off by the other fruit will hasten ripening.

2 slices (rashers) bacon, rind removed, meat finely chopped

2 cups (10 oz/315 g) self-rising flour

1 cup (4 oz/125 g) shredded Cheddar cheese

3 tablespoons finely chopped Italian (flatleaf) parsley

2 eggs, lightly beaten

1 cup (8 fl oz/250 ml) milk

¼ cup (2 oz/60 g) butter, melted

1 avocado, peeled, stoned, and finely chopped

❖ Preheat oven to 400°F (200°C/Gas Mark 5). Grease twelve standard (½-cup) muffin cups or line them with parchment (baking) paper cases.

❖ In a dry frying pan over medium heat, cook the chopped bacon, stirring, until well browned. Set aside to cool.

❖ In a large mixing bowl, sift the flour. Stir through the shredded Cheddar and parsley. Make a well in the center.

❖ In a small mixing bowl, combine the eggs, milk, and butter. Add all at once to the flour mixture together with the cooled bacon and chopped avocado. Stir until just moistened (the batter should be lumpy).

❖ Spoon batter into prepared muffin cups, filling them two-thirds full.

❖ Bake until golden brown and a wooden skewer or toothpick inserted into the center of a muffin comes out clean, 15–20 minutes. Remove from oven and cool in pan for 5 minutes. Serve warm, or transfer to a wire rack to cool.

pear, blue cheese, and walnut mini muffins

makes 24 mini muffins

These muffins, with their sophisticated combination of flavors, are perfect to serve with drinks or as finger food for a party.

2 cups (10 oz/315 g) self-rising flour

1 cup (4 oz/125 g) chopped walnuts

4 oz (125 g) soft blue cheese

1 cup (8 fl oz/250 ml) milk

2 eggs, lightly beaten

1/3 cup (3 oz/90 g) butter, melted

1 firm but ripe pear, peeled, cored, and finely chopped

✧ Preheat oven to 400°F (200°C/Gas Mark 5). Grease 24 mini muffin cups or line them with parchment (baking) paper cases.

✧ In a large mixing bowl, sift the flour. Stir through half of the walnuts. Make a well in the center.

✧ In a mixing bowl, mash the blue cheese with a fork. Gradually add the milk and mix until smooth. Add the beaten eggs and butter. Add all at once to the flour mixture together with the chopped pear. Stir until just moistened (the batter should be lumpy).

✧ Spoon batter into prepared muffin cups, filling them two-thirds full. Sprinkle with the remaining chopped walnuts.

✧ Bake until golden brown and a wooden skewer or toothpick inserted into the center of a muffin comes out clean, 15–20 minutes. Remove from oven and cool in pan for 5 minutes. Serve warm, or transfer to a wire rack to cool.

pumpkin and zucchini
soy milk muffins

makes 12 standard muffins

For use in cooking, choose
small, sweet varieties of
pumpkin with thick flesh
and a small seed cavity, such
as Sugar Pie, Baby Bear, or
Cheese varieties. Butternut
squash is also suitable. This
recipe uses soy milk, making
it suitable for those who
cannot tolerate cows' milk.

8 oz (250 g) pumpkin, seeded, peeled, and cubed

2 cups (10 oz/315 g) self-rising flour

1 teaspoon baking powder

1 egg, lightly beaten

1 cup (8 fl oz/250 ml) soy milk

1/3 cup (3 oz/90 g) butter, melted

1 medium zucchini (courgette), shredded

◈ Steam or microwave the pumpkin until tender when pierced with a fork. Cool, then mash.

◈ Preheat oven to 400°F (200°C/Gas Mark 5). Grease twelve standard (½-cup) muffin cups or line them with parchment (baking) paper cases.

◈ In a large mixing bowl, sift together the flour and baking powder. Make a well in the center.

◈ In a small mixing bowl, combine the egg, soy milk, butter, and shredded zucchini. Add all at once to the flour mixture together with the mashed pumpkin. Stir until just moistened (the batter should be lumpy).

◈ Spoon batter into prepared muffin cups, filling them two-thirds full.

◈ Bake until golden brown and a wooden skewer or toothpick inserted into the center of a muffin comes out clean, 15–20 minutes. Remove from oven and cool in pan for 5 minutes. Serve warm, or transfer to a wire rack to cool.

tomato and basil muffins with goats' cheese

makes 12 standard muffins

Tomato and basil are
a classic combination. Make
these muffins in summer,
when these two ingredients
are at their best.

2 cups (10 oz/315 g) self-rising flour

1/2 teaspoon baking powder

2 eggs, lightly beaten

1 cup (8 fl oz/250 ml) milk

1/4 cup (2 oz/60 g) butter, melted

3 oz (90 g) goats' cheese, crumbled

2 vine-ripened tomatoes, peeled, seeded, and chopped

3 tablespoons finely shredded fresh basil

⬥ Preheat oven to 400°F (200°C/Gas Mark 5). Grease twelve standard (½-cup) muffin cups or line them with parchment (baking) paper cases.

⬥ In a large mixing bowl, sift together the flour and baking powder. Make a well in the center.

⬥ In a small mixing bowl, combine the eggs, milk, and butter. Add all at once to the flour mixture together with the crumbled goats' cheese, tomato, and basil. Stir until just moistened (the batter should be lumpy).

⬥ Spoon batter into prepared muffin cups, filling them two-thirds full.

⬥ Bake until golden brown and a wooden skewer or toothpick inserted into the center of a muffin comes out clean, 15–20 minutes. Remove from oven and cool in pan for 5 minutes. Serve warm, or transfer to a wire rack to cool.

recipe hint

To peel tomatoes, cut an X in one end and place in a heat-proof bowl. Pour over boiling water to cover and leave for a few minutes. Using tongs, remove and set aside until cool enough to handle. The skin should peel away easily. (Note that this method will only work with ripe tomatoes.)

olive, parmesan, and sage muffins

makes 12 standard muffins

Parmesan is a pale yellow cows' milk cheese with a tangy, salty flavor. True Parmesan, a trademarked brand known as Parmigiano-Reggiano, is produced only in the Emilia-Romagna region of Italy to stringent standards that are protected by law. Generic Parmesan, or another hard cheese such as Romano, may be substituted.

2 cups (10 oz/315 g) self-rising flour

1 cup (3 1/2 oz/100 g) grated Parmesan

1/3 cup (2 oz/60 g) chopped black olives

1/3 cup (2 oz/60 g) chopped green olives

3 tablespoons chopped fresh sage leaves

2 eggs, lightly beaten

1 cup (8 fl oz/250 ml) buttermilk

1/3 cup (3 oz/90 ml) light olive oil

12 sage leaves, extra

◈ Preheat oven to 400°F (200°C/Gas Mark 5). Grease twelve standard (½-cup) muffin cups or line them with parchment (baking) paper cases.

◈ In a large mixing bowl, sift the flour. Stir through the Parmesan, olives, and sage leaves. Make a well in the center.

◈ In a small mixing bowl, combine the beaten eggs, buttermilk, and oil. Add all at once to flour mixture and stir until just moistened (the batter should be lumpy).

◈ Spoon batter into prepared muffin cups, filling them two-thirds full. Top each muffin with a sage leaf, pushing it a little into the batter.

◈ Bake until golden brown and a wooden skewer or toothpick inserted into the center of a muffin comes out clean, 15–20 minutes. Remove from oven and cool in pan for 5 minutes. Serve warm, or transfer to a wire rack to cool.

food fact

"Light" or "mild" olive oil is so called not because it is lower in fat or calories, but because of its lighter taste and color. These factors make it more suited to recipes for which the distinctive, fruity flavor of extra-virgin olive oil would be too strong.

mozzarella, ham, and sesame seed mini muffins

makes 24 mini muffins

Mozzarella is a pale, mild cheese originally made from buffalos' milk, now more usually from cows' milk. It is best known as the topping on pizzas. If possible, buy fresh mozzarella, which is sold surrounded by its whey, rather than the rubbery, pre-packed variety found in supermarket dairy sections.

2 cups (10 oz/315 g) self-rising flour

$1/2$ teaspoon baking powder

3 oz (90 g) diced mozzarella cheese

3 oz (90 g) finely chopped fully cooked ham

1 stick celery, finely diced

2 tablespoons chopped chives

1 tablespoon sesame seeds

2 eggs, lightly beaten

1 cup (8 fl oz/250 ml) milk

$1/3$ cup (3 oz/90 g) butter, melted

1 tablespoon sesame seeds, extra

◈ Preheat oven to 400°F (200°C/Gas Mark 5). Grease twenty-four mini muffin cups or line them with parchment (baking) paper cases.

◈ In a large mixing bowl, sift together the flour and baking powder. Stir through the cheese, ham, celery, chives, and sesame seeds. Make a well in the center.

◈ In a small mixing bowl, combine the eggs, milk, and melted butter. Add all at once to the flour mixture and stir until just moistened (the batter should be lumpy).

◈ Spoon batter into prepared muffin cups, filling them two-thirds full. Sprinkle with the extra sesame seeds.

◈ Bake until golden brown and a wooden skewer or toothpick inserted into the center of a muffin comes out clean, 12–15 minutes. Remove from oven and cool in pan for 5 minutes. Serve warm, or transfer to a wire rack to cool.

potato
and herb
muffins

makes 12 standard muffins

Potatoes add moisture,
flavor, and a slightly chewy
texture to these muffins.
They go well with roasted
meats and vegetables.

12 oz (350 g) potatoes, peeled and chopped
(2 medium potatoes)

2 cups (10 oz/315 g) self-rising flour

1 teaspoon baking powder

1 cup (4 oz/125 g) shredded Swiss cheese

2 tablespoons chopped chives

1 tablespoon chopped fresh dill

1 tablespoon chopped fresh oregano

1 tablespoon chopped Italian (flatleaf) parsley

1 egg, lightly beaten

1 cup (8 fl oz/250 ml) milk

1/4 cup (2 oz/60 g) butter, melted

◈ Preheat oven to 400°F (200°C/Gas Mark 5). Grease twelve standard (½-cup) muffin cups or line them with parchment (baking) paper cases.

◈ Boil or microwave the potatoes until tender when pierced with a sharp knife. Drain, mash, and set aside to cool.

◈ In a large mixing bowl, sift together the flour and baking powder. Stir through the cheese, chives, and herbs. Make a well in the center.

◈ In a small mixing bowl, combine the beaten egg, milk, butter, and cooled mashed potato. Add all at once to the flour mixture and stir until just moistened (the batter should be lumpy).

◈ Spoon batter into prepared muffin cups, filling them two-thirds full.

◈ Bake until golden brown and a wooden skewer or toothpick inserted into the center of a muffin comes out clean, 12–15 minutes. Remove from oven and cool in pan for 5 minutes. Serve warm, or transfer to a wire rack to cool.

bacon and apple muffins

makes 12 standard muffins

These rich muffins are a great choice for breakfast. To put warm, just-baked muffins on the breakfast table with a minimum of fuss, see page 10.

3 slices (rashers) bacon, rind removed

2 cups (10 oz/315 g) self-rising flour

½ teaspoon baking powder

2 tablespoons chopped parsley

1 tablespoon fresh thyme leaves

2 eggs, lightly beaten

1 cup (8 fl oz/250 ml) light (single) cream

⅓ cup (2¾ oz/80 ml) vegetable oil

1 apple, peeled, cored, and finely chopped

❖ Preheat oven to 400°F (200°C/Gas Mark 5). Grease twelve standard (½-cup) muffin cups or line them with parchment (baking) paper cases.

❖ In a dry frying pan or under a broiler (griller), cook the bacon until well browned and crisp. Cool, then crumble the bacon.

❖ In a large mixing bowl, sift together the flour and baking powder. Stir through the parsley and thyme. Make a well in the center.

❖ In a small mixing bowl, combine the eggs, cream, and oil. Add all at once to the flour mixture together with the crumbled bacon and chopped apple. Stir until just moistened (the batter should be lumpy).

❖ Spoon batter into prepared muffin cups, filling them two-thirds full.

❖ Bake until golden brown and a wooden skewer or toothpick inserted into the center of a muffin comes out clean, 12–15 minutes. Remove from oven and cool in pan for 5 minutes. Serve warm, or transfer to a wire rack to cool.

gouda, tomato, and parsley muffins

makes 12 standard muffins

Mild Gouda cheese, usually made from cows' milk, is encased in red wax. Its taste is similar to that of Edam, though less tangy.

2 cups (10 oz/315 g) self-rising flour

1/2 teaspoon baking powder

1 cup (5 1/2 oz/160 g) diced Gouda cheese

3 tablespoons chopped Italian (flatleaf) parsley

2 eggs, lightly beaten

1/2 cup (4 fl oz/125 ml) sour cream

1/2 cup (4 fl oz/125 ml) milk

1/3 cup (3 oz/90 g) butter, melted

2 plum (Roma) tomatoes, peeled, seeded, and chopped

❖ Preheat oven to 400°F (200°C/Gas Mark 5). Grease twelve standard (½-cup) muffin cups or line them with parchment (baking) paper cases.

❖ In a large mixing bowl, sift the flour and baking powder. Stir through the Gouda and parsley. Make a well in the center.

❖ In a small mixing bowl, combine the beaten eggs, sour cream, milk, and butter. Add all at once to the flour mixture together with the tomato. Stir until just moistened (the batter should be lumpy).

❖ Spoon batter into prepared muffin cups, filling them two-thirds full.

❖ Bake until golden brown and a wooden skewer or toothpick inserted into the center of a muffin comes out clean, 15–20 minutes. Remove from oven and cool in pan for 5 minutes. Serve warm, or transfer to a wire rack to cool.

food fact

Roma tomatoes, also known as plum or egg tomatoes, have a meaty, flavorful flesh. As their name suggests, they are popular in Italy, where they feature in salads and are favored for use in pasta sauces. If Roma tomatoes are not available, other varieties may be used instead. Vine-ripened tomatoes will provide the best flavor, but underripe fruit will ripen if left in a sunny place for a few days. Store ripe tomatoes at room temperature for up to 3 days.

part
Two

quickbreads

quickbread basics

sweet quickbreads

savory quickbreads

quickbread
basics

M uffins are just one type of quickbread. Others include tea loaves, pancakes, waffles, scones (biscuits), and coffee cakes. They are known as quickbreads because they are assembled with little effort and don't depend on slow-rising yeast to develop their volume. Instead, they use quick-acting chemical leaveners—baking powder and baking soda (bicarbonate of soda).

Depending on the final result, a quickbread begins either as a semi-liquid, somewhat flowing batter or a dough. Batters are too runny to hold a shape, so they must be baked in molds such as loaf tins, cupcake pans, or waffle irons. Doughs such as that for scones may be rolled and cut with a sharp cutter or knife, or dropped from a spoon to form irregular mounds.

Quickbreads are a boon because they are so easy to prepare, requiring minutes of your time rather than hours. But, unlike yeast doughs, most quickbread batters and doughs can't be left to sit while you are busy elsewhere. If made with baking powder, they will begin to rise as soon as liquid is added. These mixtures should be baked as soon as possible for maximum volume, unless the recipe specifies that it is formulated to be made now and baked later.

greasing the tin

The baking tin needs only partial greasing. If you grease all the way up the sides, the edges of the loaf will rise up and create an unattractive ledge. With a pastry brush or paper towel, apply a thin layer of butter or oil across the bottom and halfway up the sides. Coat evenly and completely, but don't use too much or the loaf will be sticky.

combining ingredients

Put all the dry ingredients in a large mixing bowl. With a wooden spoon, make a well in the center, into which the liquid ingredients will be poured.

Before combining eggs with other liquid ingredients, beat them briskly with a fork. Add the other liquid ingredients and whisk until thoroughly blended. Pour into the well that you have made in the flour.

stirring batter

Use a wooden spoon to quickly and lightly stir all the ingredients together just until the flour mixture is moistened. Some floury spots will remain and the batter will be lumpy. It's better to undermix than overmix.

testing with a skewer

Bake until the batter rises nicely and is a rich, golden brown. Check that the interior is done by inserting a wooden or metal skewer into the center of the loaf; if it pulls away with no batter or crumbs attached, then remove the tin from the oven.

resting and turning out

Cool the loaf in the tin for 5 minutes or so, then turn out onto a wire rack. Hot loaves do not slice well, so allow to cool a little before slicing with a serrated knife.

sweet
quickbreads

olive oil and
caraway seed
loaf

2 cups (10 oz/315 g)
all-purpose (plain) flour

1¼ teaspoons baking powder

1 cup (8 oz/250 g) sugar

2–3 teaspoons caraway seeds

grated zest of 1 lemon

1 cup (8 fl oz/250 ml) olive oil

½ cup (4 fl oz/125 ml) milk

3 eggs, separated

◈ Preheat oven to 350°F (180°C/Gas Mark 4). Grease and flour a medium-sized cake pan or loaf tin.

◈ In a large mixing bowl, sift together the flour and baking powder. Stir through the sugar, caraway seeds, and lemon zest. Add the oil, milk, and egg yolks and beat with a wooden spoon until smooth.

◈ In a medium mixing bowl, using an electric mixer on medium to high speed, beat the egg whites until stiff peaks form, then gently fold them into the batter.

◈ Spoon batter into prepared pan and smooth the surface. Bake for about 50 minutes, or until the cake comes away from the sides of the pan and is firm and dry on the surface. Invert onto a wire rack and leave to cool. Slice and serve warm.

pine nut cake

serves 10–12

One of the most traditional of all ingredients in Italian cooking is the pine nut. Pine nuts are gathered mainly in Tuscany, along the sea shore where there are whole forests of pines. In this recipe, they are toasted to enhance their flavor.

6 oz (180 g) pine nuts

4 eggs, separated

¾ cup (6 oz/180 g) superfine (caster) sugar

⅓ cup (3 oz/90 g) butter, at room temperature

2¼ cups (10 oz/315 g) all-purpose (plain) flour

1 tablespoon confectioners' (icing) sugar, for dusting

❖ Preheat oven to 350°F (180°C/Gas Mark 4). Grease and flour a 9-inch (23-cm) springform pan.

❖ Scatter the pine nuts over a baking sheet. Place in oven and toast until they begin to color, shaking the baking sheet occasionally. Check them frequently, as they burn easily. Allow to cool, then grind 5 oz (155 g) of them in a blender or mortar and pestle, reserving the rest whole.

❖ In a bowl, beat the egg yolks with half the sugar. In another bowl, beat the remaining sugar with the butter. Gently stir the two mixtures together. Gradually add the combined mixture to the flour, mixing in a little at a time to avoid lumps forming.

❖ In a medium mixing bowl, using an electric mixer on medium to high speed, beat the egg whites until stiff peaks form. Gently fold them into the batter, taking care to retain as much air as possible. Fold the ground nuts into the batter. Spoon batter into the prepared pan and bake until a skewer inserted in the center comes out dry, about 45 minutes.

❖ Cool in pan for 5 minutes, then turn the cake out onto a wire rack. Serve warm or cool, decorated with the remaining whole pine nuts and dusted with sifted confectioners' sugar.

coconut cupcakes

makes about 24

These delicate little cakes, fragrant with coconut, are simple to make and favorites with children of all ages. If you like, dress them up with your choice of icing (see page 205) and a sprinkling of nuts or extra coconut.

4 eggs

2/3 cup (4 1/2 oz/140 g) sugar

1 1/4 cups (4 oz/125 g) all-purpose (plain) flour

1 teaspoon baking powder

3/4 cup (2 1/2 oz/75 g) flaked (desiccated) coconut

1/2 cup (4 oz/125 g) butter, melted

❖ Preheat oven to 415°F (210°C/Gas Mark 5). Grease twenty-four ½-cup cupcake or muffin molds or line them with parchment (baking) paper cases.

❖ Combine the eggs and sugar in a large bowl. Beat until the mixture is thick and pale and forms a ribbon.

❖ Sift together the flour and baking powder and fold into the egg mixture alternately with the coconut. Fold in the melted butter with the last batch. Chill for 25 minutes, or until the mixture thickens slightly.

❖ Divide the mixture among the cupcake pans, filling them two-thirds full. Bake for 5 minutes. Reduce the oven temperature to 400°F (200°C/Gas Mark 6) and bake for 5–7 minutes, or until risen and golden.

❖ Remove from the oven and cool in pan for 5 minutes, then turn out onto a wire rack. Serve warm, or allow to cool completely, then ice.

tempting toppings

white chocolate drizzle

In a small saucepan or microwave oven, melt ½ cup (3 oz/90 g) chopped white chocolate or choc chips and 1 teaspoon vegetable shortening. Stir to combine, then drizzle over cupcakes.

vanilla icing

In a small saucepan or microwave oven, melt 3 tablespoons butter. Remove from heat. Stir in 2¼ cups (9 oz/280 g) sifted confectioners' (icing) sugar, 1 teaspoon vanilla extract (essence), and enough milk (1–2 tablespoons) to give a spreadable consistency. If icing becomes too stiff, add hot water, a few drops at a time, and stir until smooth. Using a palette knife, swirl over tops of cupcakes.

fruit and chocolate chip cupcakes

makes about 24

These cupcakes are like miniature fruit cakes with the addition of chocolate. They travel well, so are good for children's lunch boxes or picnics.

4 eggs

2/3 cup (5½ oz/160 g) sugar

1¼ cups (6½ oz/190 g) all-purpose (plain) flour

1 teaspoon baking powder

2/3 cup (5 oz/155 g) butter, melted

1/3 cup (2 oz/60 g) chopped dried apricots

1 tablespoon finely chopped candied (glacé) green cherries

2 tablespoons finely chopped candied (glacé) red cherries

1 tablespoon dried currants

1 tablespoon finely chopped blanched almonds

½ cup (3 oz/90 g) sweet (milk) chocolate chips

1 tablespoon chopped candied (glacé) ginger

❖ Preheat oven to 400°F (200°C/Gas Mark 6). Grease twenty-four mini cupcake pans.

❖ Using an electric mixer on medium to high speed, beat the eggs and sugar until thick and pale, about 5 minutes. Fold in all of the remaining ingredients. Cover, then refrigerate for 25 minutes.

❖ Place 1 tablespoon of the mixture into each cupcake mold. Bake for 15 minutes, or until cooked through and a skewer inserted in the middle of one of the cakes comes out clean. Cool in the pan for 2–3 minutes before turning out onto a wire rack to cool completely.

❖ Serve warm or cool.

recipe variations

Experiment with different types of fruit and nuts in this recipe. Replace the currants with dates and the almonds with hazelnuts, or try adding figs and walnuts or pecans.

coconut and raspberry cupcakes

makes 32

Each of these little cakes contains a spoonful of raspberry jam in the center. Raspberry and coconut are a delicious combination, but you could also try other flavors of jam, such as strawberry, blueberry, apricot, or your favorite type of marmalade.

4 eggs

2/3 cup (5 1/2 oz/165 g) sugar

1 1/4 cups (6 1/2 oz/190 g) all-purpose (plain) flour

1 teaspoon baking powder

2/3 cup (2 oz/60 g) flaked (desiccated) coconut

1/2 cup (4 oz/125 g) butter, melted

1/4 cup (3 oz/90 g) raspberry preserves (jam)

confectioners' (icing) sugar, for dusting

✧ Preheat oven to 415°F (210°C/Gas Mark 6). Grease thirty-two ½-cup cupcake or muffin molds or line them with parchment (baking) paper cases. (If you do not have enough pans, the cakes may be cooked in batches.)

✧ In a large bowl, using an electric mixer on medium to high speed, beat the eggs and sugar until the mixture is thick and pale and forms a ribbon. Sift together the flour and baking powder and fold into the egg mixture alternately with the coconut. Fold in the melted butter, then chill in the refrigerator for 25 minutes.

✧ Place 2 teaspoons of the batter into each prepared mold, dot ½ teaspoon of preserves in the center, then top with another 2 teaspoons of batter so that each mold is three-fourths full. Bake for 5 minutes, then reduce the heat to 400°F (200°C/Gas Mark 6) and bake for a further 5–7 minutes, or until risen and golden. Turn out onto wire racks to cool completely.

✧ Dust with sifted confectioners' sugar and serve.

financiers

makes 12

These rich, buttery cakes
made with ground almonds
are a French specialty.

4½ oz (140 g) whole blanched almonds

1½ cups (7 oz/220 g) confectioners' (icing) sugar

½ cup (2½ oz/75 g) all-purpose (plain) flour, sifted

5 egg whites

¾ cup (6 oz/185 g) sweet (unsalted) butter,
melted and cooled

2–3 poached or canned pear halves, thinly sliced

◈ Preheat oven to 425°F (220°C/Gas Mark 7). Grease twelve standard (½-cup) muffin cups.

◈ Toast the almonds on a baking sheet until golden, 5–7 minutes, shaking them occasionally. Remove from oven, cool, then place in a food processor and process until finely ground.

◈ In a medium mixing bowl, combine the ground almonds with the sugar and flour. Stir in the egg whites and mix until well blended. Add the melted butter and stir to combine thoroughly.

◈ Spoon the mixture into the prepared muffin cups, filling them three-fourths full. Lay a few slices of pear on top of each.

◈ Bake for 15–20 minutes, or until each cake is peaked and golden and a skewer inserted in the center comes out clean.

◈ Turn off the oven and let the cakes remain inside with the door slightly ajar for 5 minutes. Cool in the pans for 5 minutes before turning out onto a wire rack to cool completely.

◈ Serve warm or cold.

makes 8–10 scones

*⅔ cup (5½ fl oz/170 ml)
crème fraîche*

*2 tablespoons confectioners'
(icing) sugar*

*2 cups (10 oz/315 g)
all-purpose (plain) flour*

*3 tablespoons granulated
sugar, plus extra for dusting*

*1¼ teaspoons cream of
tartar*

*1 teaspoon baking soda
(bicarbonate of soda)*

½ teaspoon salt

*¼ cup (2 oz/60 g) chilled
butter, cut into pieces*

1 egg, beaten

*½ cup (4 fl oz/125 ml) heavy
(double) cream*

*¼ cup (1⅕ oz/45 g) dried
currants*

jam or jelly of your choice

❖ Preheat oven to 400°F (200°C/Gas Mark 5). Grease and flour a baking sheet.

❖ In a bowl, lightly whisk together the crème fraîche and confectioners' sugar until soft peaks form. Cover and refrigerate until needed.

❖ In a large mixing bowl, sift together the flour, 3 tablespoons granulated sugar, cream of tartar, baking soda, and salt. Add the butter and, using a pastry blender, 2 forks, or your fingertips, cut it in until the mixture forms large crumbs. Add the egg, cream, and currants. Stir together with a wooden spoon until a soft dough forms. Do not overmix, or the dough will toughen.

❖ Turn the dough out onto a floured work surface and knead briefly just until the dough holds together. Pat it out to a ½–¾ inch (12 mm–2 cm) thickness. Using a floured 2½-inch (6-cm) round biscuit cutter, cut out rounds and place them about ¾ inch (2 cm) apart on the prepared baking sheet. Dust lightly with the extra granulated sugar.

❖ Bake until golden brown, about 12 minutes. Remove from the oven and serve immediately with the whipped crème fraîche and jam or jelly.

currant scones
with crème fraîche

blueberry hotcakes

makes 6

2 cups (10 oz/315 g) all-purpose (plain) flour

2 teaspoons baking powder

1 teaspoon baking soda (bicarbonate of soda)

⅓ cup (3 oz/90 g) superfine (caster) sugar

2 eggs

1¼ cups (10 fl oz/300 ml) milk

⅓ cup (3 oz/90 g) butter, melted

2 cups (8 oz/250 g) fresh blueberries

extra butter, for greasing

crème fraîche, to serve

❖ In a large mixing bowl, sift together the flour, baking powder, and baking soda. Stir through the sugar. Make a well in the center.

❖ In a small mixing bowl, whisk together the eggs, milk, and butter. Add all at once to the flour. Gradually whisk in the liquid just until all the ingredients are combined. Thin with a little extra milk if the batter is too thick. Fold in the blueberries.

❖ Grease a nonstick frying pan with butter. Over low heat, warm the pan. When hot, add ½ cup (4 fl oz/125 ml) of the batter. Using a spatula, spread evenly into a pancake about 6 inches (15 cm) across. Cook until bubbles appear on the surface. Turn and cook a further 2–3 minutes. Keep warm in a low oven while cooking the rest of the batter in the same way.

❖ Serve warm with crème fraîche.

215

butterscotch and currant pinwheels

makes 12 pinwheels

½ cup (2½ oz/75 g) dried currants

2 tablespoons brandy or apple juice

⅓ cup (3 oz/90 g) butter,
at room temperature

⅓ cup (2¼ oz/65 g) firmly packed
brown sugar

2 cups (10 oz/315 g)
self-rising flour

2 tablespoons (1 oz/30 g)
chilled butter, chopped

¾ cup (6 fl oz/185 ml) milk

❖ Preheat oven to 415°F (210°C/Gas Mark 5). Grease a baking sheet.

❖ In a small bowl, combine the currants and brandy or juice. Set aside to soften while making the dough.

❖ In another small bowl, combine the softened butter and brown sugar to form a paste. Set aside.

❖ In a large mixing bowl, sift the flour. Using fingertips, rub the chilled butter into the flour. Make a well in the center.

❖ Add most of the milk to the flour mixture. Using a flat-bladed knife, mix to a soft dough, adding remaining milk if necessary. Turn out onto a floured surface and knead quickly and gently into a smooth ball. Pat or roll out into a 12- x 9- inch (30- x 23- cm) rectangle.

❖ Using a metal spatula, spread the butter and sugar mixture over the dough, leaving a ¾-inch (2-cm) border on the long sides. Drain the currants and scatter over the dough.

❖ Roll the dough from the long side, sealing the edge with a little milk. Place on a baking sheet, cover with plastic wrap, and refrigerate for 20 minutes.

❖ Using a sharp knife, cut the chilled dough into 12 even slices. Place the slices, cut-side up and close together, onto the prepared baking sheet. Bake for 12–15 minutes, or until golden brown. Serve warm.

nut bread

**makes 1 large loaf,
2 small loaves, or
6 mini loaves**

*3 cups (14 oz/450 g)
all-purpose flour*

*1 cup (8 oz/250 g)
sugar*

*1 tablespoon
baking powder*

½ teaspoon salt

*¼ teaspoon baking
soda (bicarbonate
of soda)*

1 beaten egg

*1⅔ cups (13 fl oz/
410 ml) milk*

*¼ cup (2 fl oz/60 ml)
vegetable oil*

*¾ teaspoon almond
extract (essence)*

*¾ cup (3 oz/90 g)
chopped pecans
or other nuts*

❖ Preheat oven to 350°F (180°C/Gas Mark 4). Grease one
9- x 5- x 3-inch (23- x 13- x 8-cm) loaf pan, two 7½- x
3½- x 2-inch (19- x 9- x 5-cm) loaf pans, or six 4½- x 2½- x
1½-inch (11- x 6- x 4-cm) individual loaf pans; set aside.

❖ In a large mixing bowl, sift together flour, sugar, baking
powder, salt, and baking soda. Make a well in the center.

❖ In a small mixing bowl, combine the egg, milk,
oil, and almond extract. Add all at once to
the flour mixture, stirring until just combined
(the batter should be lumpy). Stir in the nuts.

❖ Pour batter into prepared pan(s). Bake for about
1–1¼ hours for the 9- x 5- x 3-inch (23- x 13- x 8-cm) loaf,
40–45 minutes for the 7½- x 3½- x 2-inch (19- x 9- x 5-cm)
loaves, and 30–35 minutes for the 4½- x 2½- x 1½-inch
(11- x 6- x 4-cm) loaves. When done, a toothpick inserted
near the center of a loaf will come out clean.

❖ Cool in the pan(s) for 10 minutes. Remove from pan(s)
and transfer to wire racks to cool completely. Wrap in
plastic wrap and store overnight before slicing.

strawberry shortcakes

makes 8

SHORTCAKE

*2 cups (10 oz/315 g)
all-purpose (plain) flour*

2 tablespoons sugar

2 teaspoons baking powder

½ teaspoon salt

*2 tablespoons chilled
butter, cut into pieces*

*1½ teaspoons grated
lemon zest*

*¾ cup (6 fl oz/185 ml)
heavy (double) cream*

¼ cup (2 fl oz/60 ml) milk

*2 tablespoons butter, at
room temperature*

FILLING

*8 oz (250 g) strawberries,
hulled and chopped*

¼ cup (2 oz/60 g) sugar

1 teaspoon lemon juice

*1 cup (8 fl oz/250 ml) heavy
(double) cream, whipped*

*extra strawberries, halved,
to decorate*

❖ Preheat oven to 400°F (200°C/Gas Mark 6). Grease a baking sheet.

❖ In a large bowl, sift together the flour, sugar, baking powder, and salt. Add the chilled butter and lemon zest and, using your fingertips, rub into flour until mixture resembles coarse crumbs. Gradually stir in enough cream to make a soft dough.

❖ On a floured surface, quickly form dough into a ball. Roll or pat it out to ½ inch (1 cm) thick. Cut out 3-inch (7.5-cm) rounds and arrange on baking sheet. Form scraps gently into a ball, roll out, and cut more rounds. Brush tops of rounds lightly with milk. Bake until puffed and golden, 15–20 minutes.

❖ Split cakes horizontally with a knife. While still warm, spread the halves with the softened butter.

❖ For filling, combine the strawberries, sugar, and lemon juice in a small saucepan over moderate heat. Bring to a boil, then cook, stirring constantly, for 5 minutes. Transfer to a bowl and cool completely.

❖ Cover the bottom half of each cake with strawberry mixture and some of the cream. Add the top halves of the cakes and more cream, and decorate each cake with a half-strawberry. Serve immediately.

scandinavian
oatmeal cake

serves 10

1 cup (3½ oz/100 g) rolled oats

1¼ cups (10 fl oz/315 ml) boiling water

1 cup (6 oz/185 g) packed brown sugar

1 cup (8 oz/250 g) granulated (white) sugar

½ cup (4 oz/125 g) butter, melted

2 eggs

1⅓ cups (6½ oz/200 g) all-purpose (plain) flour

1½ teaspoons ground cinnamon

¾ teaspoon baking powder

½ teaspoon salt

TOPPING

½ cup (3 oz/90 g) packed brown sugar

½ cup (1½ oz/45 g) walnut halves

½ cup (¾ oz/20 g) freshly grated or canned coconut

½ cup (4 oz/125 g) butter, melted

½ teaspoon ground cinnamon

◈ Preheat oven to 350°F (180°C/Gas Mark 4). Grease a 9-inch (23-cm) springform cake pan and line with parchment (baking) or waxed (greaseproof) paper.

◈ Place the oats in a heatproof bowl, pour the boiling water over, and stir. In another bowl, combine the brown sugar, granulated sugar, and melted butter. Beat in the eggs, one at a time, beating well with a wooden spoon after each addition. Add the oat mixture and stir until well blended. Sift together the flour, cinnamon, baking powder, and salt. Add to the oat mixture and stir until combined.

◈ Spoon the batter into the prepared pan and smooth the top. Bake for 1 hour, or until a skewer inserted into the center comes out clean. Cool in the pan on a wire rack for at least 10 minutes before releasing the sides of the pan.

◈ For the topping, in a bowl, combine the sugar, walnuts, coconut, butter, and cinnamon and spread over the top of the cake. Place under a preheated broiler (griller), about 4 inches (10 cm) from the heat, for 4–5 minutes, or until the topping is golden and bubbling.

◈ Serve warm or at room temperature.

banana–cream cheese cake

serves 8–10

4 oz (125 g) cream cheese, at room temperature

½ cup (4 oz/125 g) butter, at room temperature

1 cup (6 oz/185 g) packed brown sugar

2 eggs

2 large ripe bananas, mashed

2 cups (10 oz/315 g) all-purpose (plain) flour

1 tablespoon baking powder

¼ cup (1½ oz/45 g) ground almonds

ICING

8 oz (250 g) cream cheese, at room temperature

1 cup (5 oz/150 g) confectioners' (icing) sugar

1 large ripe banana

2 tablespoons lemon juice

✧ Preheat oven to 375°F (190°C/Gas Mark 5). Grease a 4- x 8-inch (10- x 20-cm) loaf pan.

✧ In a large mixing bowl, combine the cream cheese, butter, and brown sugar. Using an electric mixer on medium to high speed, beat until creamy. Add the eggs, one at a time, beating well after each addition. Stir in the banana. Sift together the flour and baking powder and stir into the mixture. Fold in the nuts.

✧ Spoon batter into prepared pan and bake for 1 hour, or until a skewer inserted into the center comes out clean. Cool in pan for 5 minutes, then turn out onto a wire rack. Allow to cool completely before icing.

✧ For the icing, using an electric mixer on medium to high speed, beat the cream cheese and confectioners' sugar until smooth. Using a palette knife, spread the icing over the top of the cake. Peel and thinly slice the banana. Toss the slices in the lemon juice, then arrange over the top of the icing. Serve immediately.

basic biscuits

makes 10 biscuits

2 cups (10 oz/315 g)
all-purpose (plain) flour

1 tablespoon baking powder

2 teaspoons sugar

½ teaspoon cream of tartar

¼ teaspoon salt

½ cup (4 oz/125 g) chilled
vegetable shortening or butter

⅔ cup (6 fl oz/180 ml) milk

❖ Preheat oven to 415°F (210°C/Gas Mark 5).

❖ In a medium mixing bowl, sift together the flour, baking powder, sugar, cream of tartar, and salt. Using a pastry blender or your fingertips, cut in shortening or butter until mixture resembles coarse crumbs. Make a well in the center; add milk all at once. Using a fork, stir just until the dough clings together.

❖ Turn dough out onto a lightly floured surface. Knead briefly until nearly smooth. Roll or pat out to a ½-inch (1-cm) thickness. Cut out rounds with a floured 2½-inch (6-cm) biscuit cutter. Form scraps gently into a ball, roll out, and cut more rounds.

❖ Arrange dough rounds on an ungreased baking sheet. Bake for 10–12 minutes, or until golden and well risen. Serve warm.

pikelets

makes 14–16 pikelets

1⅓ cups (6½ oz/200 g)
all-purpose (plain) flour

¼ cup (2 oz/60 g) sugar

1 teaspoon baking powder

½ teaspoon baking soda
(bicarbonate of soda)

½ teaspoon salt

1 beaten egg

1 cup (8 fl oz/250 ml)
buttermilk

⅓ cup (3 oz/90 g) butter or
margarine, melted

butter, honey, and/or jam,
to serve

❖ In a medium mixing bowl, sift together the flour, sugar, baking powder, baking soda, and salt. Make a well in the center. In a small mixing bowl, combine the egg, buttermilk, and melted butter or margarine and add all at once to the flour mixture. Stir just until moistened. (The batter should be lumpy.)

❖ For each pikelet, spoon 2 rounded tablespoons of the batter onto a lightly greased hot griddle or heavy frying pan. Using the back of a spoon, spread the batter out into a circle about 3½ inches (9 cm) across. Cook a few pikelets at a time, leaving enough room to flip them easily. Cook until pikelets have slightly dry edges and surfaces dotted with bubbles, about 3 minutes. Using a spatula, flip the pikelets and cook until the underside is golden, about 2 minutes more. Repeat with remaining batter. Serve warm with butter, honey, and/or jam.

apricot-prune coffee cake

STREUSEL

1/4 cup (2 oz/60 g) packed brown sugar

2 tablespoons all-purpose (plain) flour

1 teaspoon ground cinnamon

2 tablespoons chilled butter

CAKE

1/2 cup (3 oz/90 g) dried apricots, quartered

1/2 cup (3 oz/90 g) dried prunes, quartered

1 1/2 cups (7 oz/220 g) all-purpose (plain) flour

3/4 cup (6 oz/185 g) granulated (white) sugar

2 teaspoons baking powder

1/4 teaspoon salt

1 egg, lightly beaten

2/3 cup (5 1/2 fl oz/170 ml) milk

1/4 cup (2 fl oz/60 ml) vegetable oil

1/2 teaspoon vanilla extract (essence)

◈ Preheat oven to 375°F (190°C/Gas Mark 4). Grease a 9- x 12-inch (18- x 30-cm) round cake pan and line base with parchment (baking) paper.

◈ For streusel, in a small bowl, combine brown sugar, flour, and cinnamon. With a pastry blender or fingertips, cut in butter until mixture resembles coarse crumbs.

◈ Place dried apricots and prunes in a small bowl; add boiling water to cover. Stand for 5 minutes, then drain.

◈ Meanwhile, in a large mixing bowl, stir together the flour, granulated sugar, baking powder, and salt. Make a well in the center. In a medium mixing bowl, combine the egg, milk, oil, and vanilla. Stir until well blended. Add egg mixture to flour mixture. Mix well.

◈ Spread two-thirds of batter into the prepared pan. Arrange drained apricots and prunes atop cake batter. Dollop remaining batter atop the fruit. Sprinkle with the streusel topping. Bake for 30–35 minutes, or until a wooden or metal skewer inserted into the center comes out clean. Serve warm.

recipe **hint**

Plenty of crumbly streusel tops this coffee cake, which is perfect served first thing in the morning or for dessert after dinner. Be sure to cut the dried fruits into bite-size pieces; this ensures that they disperse evenly through the dough. Use kitchen scissors, oiling the blades first so the sticky fruit is released easily.

toasted coconut and banana bread

makes 1 loaf (18 servings)

Finely shredded coconut adds a sweet crunch to this moist, flavorful bread. Toast a slice for breakfast or serve it chilled with a main-dish salad for lunch.

1½ cups (3½ oz/100 g) flaked (desiccated) coconut

1¾ cups (9 oz/270 g) all-purpose (plain) flour

½ cup (4 oz/125 g) sugar

2 teaspoons baking powder

½ teaspoon baking soda (bicarbonate of soda)

¼ teaspoon salt

2 eggs, lightly beaten

1 cup (8 oz/250 g) mashed ripe bananas (2–3 medium bananas)

⅓ cup (3 fl oz/90 g) vegetable oil

2 tablespoons milk

1 teaspoon vanilla extract (essence)

✧ Preheat oven to 350°F (180°C/Gas Mark 4). Grease a 9- x 5- x 3-inch (23- x 13- x 8-cm) loaf pan; set aside.

✧ To toast the coconut, spread it on a medium-sized baking sheet. Place in preheated oven and toast just until the coconut turns golden. Watch carefully to ensure that it doesn't brown too much. Halfway through baking, stir to expose all the flakes to heat.

✧ In a large mixing bowl, sift together the flour, sugar, baking powder, baking soda, and salt. Make a well in the center. In a medium mixing bowl, combine the eggs, mashed bananas, oil, milk, and vanilla; mix well. Add all at once to the flour mixture and stir until just combined. (The batter should be lumpy.) Fold in the toasted coconut.

✧ Pour batter into prepared pan. Bake for 50–60 minutes, or until a wooden or metal skewer inserted into the center comes out clean.

✧ Remove from oven and cool in pan on a wire rack for 10 minutes. Remove cake from pan; transfer to a wire rack to cool completely. Wrap and store overnight before slicing.

ginger scones

makes eight 3-inch (8-cm) or
sixteen 2-inch (5-cm) scones

Host an afternoon tea
with a tray of these fruit-
filled scones. Serve them
warm with strawberry
preserves and thick crème
fraîche for a decidedly
civilized treat.

Scones are made in a very
similar fashion to biscuits,
although there is less
shortening in the dough.

CRÈME FRAÎCHE

¼ cup (2 fl oz/60 ml) whipping cream
(not ultrapasteurized)

¼ cup (2 fl oz/60 ml) sour cream

SCONES

2 cups (10 oz/315 g) all-purpose (plain) flour

1 tablespoon baking powder

1 tablespoon sugar

½ teaspoon salt

2 tablespoons finely chopped crystallized ginger
or candied (glacé) lemon peel, or ½ teaspoon
ground ginger

½ cup (2½ oz/75 g) dried currants or
chopped golden raisins

1¼ cups (10 fl oz/315 ml) whipping cream

milk or whipping cream, extra

strawberry preserves (jam), to serve

◈ Preheat oven to 425°F (220°C/Gas Mark 6).

◈ For crème fraîche, in a small mixing bowl, stir together whipping cream and sour cream. Cover with plastic wrap. Let stand at room temperature for 2–5 hours, or until mixture thickens, then cover and chill in the refrigerator until cold or for up to 1 week. Stir before serving.

◈ For scones, in a large mixing bowl, sift together the flour, baking powder, sugar, and salt. Stir through the crystallized ginger, candied lemon peel, or ground ginger. Stir in currants or raisins. Make a well in the center; add cream all at once. Using a fork, stir until just moistened.

◈ Turn the dough out onto a lightly floured surface. Quickly knead by gently folding and pressing dough for 10–12 strokes, or until nearly smooth. Pat or lightly roll dough out to a ½-inch (1-cm) thickness. Cut dough with a floured 2- to 3-inch (5- to 8-cm) round cookie cutter, dipping cutter into flour between cuts. Place scones 1 inch (2.5 cm) apart on a large ungreased baking sheet. Brush tops with milk or additional cream.

◈ Bake for 12–15 minutes, or until golden brown. Remove scones from baking sheet. Transfer to a wire rack and let cool for 15 minutes.

◈ To serve, split scones and spread with strawberry preserves. Top with crème fraîche.

graham cracker
tea bread

makes 1 loaf (16 servings)

This dense, full-flavored bread isn't overly sweet but has a nutty flavor from both the graham crackers (wholemeal biscuits) and the chopped pecans. Always buy the freshest nuts available, or they won't be crisp. Use slices of this loaf to make an unusual French toast.

⅓ cup (3 oz/90 g) butter, at room temperature

⅓ cup (3 oz/90 g) granulated (white) sugar

2 eggs

2⅔ cups (8 oz/250 g) fine graham cracker (wholemeal biscuit) crumbs (about 40 crackers)

½ teaspoon baking powder

½ teaspoon baking soda (bicarbonate of soda)

1 teaspoon finely shredded orange zest, plus extra to serve (optional)

¾ cup (6 fl oz/180 ml) orange juice

1 cup (4 oz/125 g) chopped pecans

½ cup (2½ oz/75 g) sifted confectioners' (icing) sugar

1–2 teaspoons orange juice

⊕ Grease and flour an 8- x 4- x 2-inch (20- x 10- x 5-cm) loaf pan. Line base with parchment (baking) paper. Preheat oven to 350ºF (180ºC/Gas Mark 4).

⊕ In a large mixing bowl, combine softened butter and granulated sugar. Using an electric mixer on medium to high speed, beat until fluffy. Add eggs, one at a time; beat until blended.

⊕ In a small mixing bowl, combine the cracker crumbs, baking powder, baking soda, and the 1 teaspoon orange zest. Alternately add crumb mixture and the ¾ cup (6 fl oz/185 ml) orange juice to butter mixture, beating on low to medium speed after each addition until just combined. Stir in pecans.

⊕ Pour batter into prepared pan. Bake for 55–60 minutes, or until a wooden or metal skewer inserted into the center comes out clean. Remove from oven and cool in pan on a wire rack for 10 minutes. Remove from pan and transfer to wire rack to cool completely. Wrap and store overnight before slicing.

⊕ Before serving, in a small mixing bowl, stir together confectioners' sugar and enough orange juice to make a smooth icing of drizzling consistency. Drizzle over the bread, then sprinkle with extra orange zest, if desired.

gingerbread

serves 8–10

1⅔ cups (13 fl oz/410 ml) light molasses (golden syrup)

⅓ cup (4 fl oz/125 ml) honey

¾ cup (6 fl oz/185 ml) grapeseed oil

1 cup (8 fl oz/250 ml) water

1 cup (6 oz/185 g) packed brown sugar

3 eggs

2 cups (10 oz/315 g) all-purpose (plain) flour

1 cup (5 oz/150 g) self-rising flour

1 teaspoon ground allspice

½ teaspoon ground cinnamon

1 teaspoon ground ginger

½ teaspoon baking soda (bicarbonate of soda)

LEMON ICING

juice of ½ lemon

¾ oz (20 g) butter, at room temperature

1¼ cups (7 oz/220 g) confectioners' (icing) sugar

◈ Preheat oven to 350°F (180°C/Gas Mark 4). Lightly grease an 8-inch (20-cm) square cake pan and line with baking (parchment) or waxed (greaseproof) paper.

◈ In a large saucepan, combine the molasses or golden syrup, honey, oil, water, and sugar. Stir over low heat until sugar is dissolved, then bring to a boil. Remove from the heat and allow to cool. Add the eggs, one at a time, and mix until smooth. Sift together the flours, spices, and baking soda, add to the liquid mixture, and stir until smooth.

◈ Spoon batter into the prepared pan. Bake for 1¼ hours, or until a skewer inserted in the center of the cake comes out clean. Let the cake rest in the pan for 10 minutes before turning out onto a wire rack to cool.

◈ For the icing, combine the lemon juice and butter in the top of a double boiler. Mix until the butter is melted and the mixture is smooth. Stir the butter mixture into the sifted confectioners' sugar, mixing until smooth. Stand the icing over hot water to thin slightly, then spread over the cooled cake as quickly as possible. Serve cut into slices.

irish teacake

serves 10–12

2⅓ cups (12 oz/350 g) dried
currants or golden raisins
(sultanas)

1 cup (8 fl oz/250 ml) cold
strong tea

1 cup (6 oz/185 g) lightly
packed brown sugar

2 cups (10 oz/315 g) self-rising
flour

1 egg, beaten

butter, to serve

❖ In a large mixing bowl, combine the fruit, tea, and sugar and leave to soak overnight at room temperature.

❖ Preheat oven to 350°F (180°C/Gas Mark 4). Grease a 9- x 4- x 3-inch (23- x 10- x 8-cm) baking pan and line with parchment (baking) or waxed (greaseproof) paper.

❖ Sift the flour into the bowl containing the currant mixture. Add the egg and mix well. Spoon batter into the prepared pan. Bake for 1½ hours, or until a skewer inserted into the center of the cake comes out clean. Remove from oven and cool in pan for 10 minutes before turning out onto a wire rack to cool completely.

❖ Serve the cake sliced and spread with butter.

poppyseed currant cake

¾ cup (6 oz/185 g) butter,
at room temperature

½ cup (4 oz/125 g) sugar

2 eggs, beaten

½ cup (4 fl oz/125 ml) milk

1½ cups (7½ oz/235 g) self-
rising flour

9 oz (270 g) dried currants
and/or golden raisins (sultanas)

¼ cup poppy seeds

❖ Preheat oven to 350°F (180°C/Gas Mark 4). Grease an 8-inch (20-cm) round cake pan and line base with parchment (baking) or waxed (greaseproof) paper.

❖ In a small mixing bowl, using an electric mixer on medium to high speed, beat together the butter and sugar until light and fluffy. Add the eggs and milk. Using a wooden spoon, mix well. (The mixture may look curdled, but will normalize once the remaining ingredients are added.) Transfer to a large mixing bowl.

❖ Sift the flour into the bowl containing the butter-and-egg mixture. Fold in dried fruit and poppy seeds.

❖ Spoon batter into prepared pan. Bake until a skewer inserted into the center of the cake comes out clean, about 1 hour. Cool in pan for 10 minutes before turning out onto a wire rack to cool completely.

multi-grain waffles

makes 3–4 waffles

For spicy fruit waffles, add 1 teaspoon ground cinnamon, 1 teaspoon ground cloves, and ½ teaspoon ground ginger to the dry ingredients. Fold ½ cup (3 oz/90 g) finely chopped dates into the batter before folding in the egg whites, and serve the waffles with maple syrup instead of fruit sauce.

RASPBERRY-PEACH SAUCE

1 cup (10 oz/315 g) red raspberry all-fruit spread or apricot preserves

1 tablespoon raspberry liqueur or orange juice

1 cup (4–5 oz/125–150 g) loose-pack frozen peaches or raspberries, thawed

WAFFLES

1 cup (5 oz/155 g) all-purpose (plain) flour

¾ cup (4½ oz/140 g) quick-cooking multi-grain cereal or muesli

1 tablespoon baking powder

¼ teaspoon salt

2 egg yolks

1 cup (8 oz/250 g) plain yogurt

¾ cup (6 fl oz/185 ml) milk

¼ cup (2 fl oz/60 ml) vegetable oil

2 egg whites

✦ For raspberry-peach sauce, in a small saucepan, heat all-fruit spread or preserves and liqueur or orange juice until fruit spread or preserves are melted. Stir in peaches or raspberries; heat through. Keep warm while preparing waffles.

✦ Preheat oven to 350°F (180°C/Gas Mark 4).

✦ For waffles, in a large mixing bowl, stir together the flour, multi-grain cereal or muesli, baking powder, and salt. Make a well in the center. In a medium mixing bowl, using a fork, beat egg yolks lightly. Beat in yogurt, milk, and oil. Add egg yolk mixture to flour mixture all at once. Stir until just combined. (The batter will be lumpy.)

✦ In a small mixing bowl, using an electric mixer on medium to high speed, beat egg whites until stiff peaks form (tips stand straight). Gently fold beaten egg whites into cereal mixture, leaving a few streaks of egg white. Do not overmix.

✦ Pour 1–1¼ cups (8–10 fl oz/250–300 ml) of batter onto grids of a lightly greased preheated waffle baker. Close lid quickly; do not open during baking. Bake according to manufacturer's directions (about 5 minutes). When done, use a fork to lift waffle off grid. Place cooked waffles on a roasting rack or wire cooling rack set on a baking sheet in the preheated oven. Repeat with remaining batter, placing each cooked waffle on the rack in the oven. (Do not stack waffles; arrange them in a single layer.) Serve warm with raspberry-peach sauce.

raisin-cinnamon apple bread

makes 1 loaf (18 servings)

Make this moist, spicy bread one day ahead, then serve it with tea, coffee, or cocoa the next afternoon. This loaf keeps well for several days.

2 cups (10 oz/315 g) all-purpose (plain) flour

1 cup (8 oz/250 g) sugar

1 1/2 teaspoons ground cinnamon

1 teaspoon baking powder

1/2 teaspoon baking soda (bicarbonate of soda)

1/2 teaspoon salt

1 cup (9 oz/280 g) applesauce or stewed, puréed apple

2 eggs, beaten

1/2 cup (4 fl oz/125 ml) vegetable oil

1/4 cup (2 fl oz/60 ml) milk

1 cup (6 oz/185 g) raisins or currants
or 1/2 cup (2 oz/60 g) chopped dried cherries
or dried cranberries

❖ Preheat oven to 350°F (180°C/Gas Mark 4). Grease a 9- x 5- x 3-inch (18- x 12 x 8-cm) loaf pan and line base with parchment (baking) paper.

❖ In a large mixing bowl, sift together the flour, sugar, cinnamon, baking powder, baking soda, and salt. Make a well in the center. In a medium mixing bowl, combine applesauce or stewed apple, eggs, oil, and milk. Add to flour mixture all at once; stir until just combined. Fold in fruit.

❖ Pour batter into prepared pan. Bake for 60–65 minutes, or until a wooden or metal skewer inserted into the center comes out clean. Remove from oven and cool in pan for 10 minutes. Remove from pan; transfer to a wire rack to cool completely. Once cool, wrap in plastic wrap and store overnight before slicing.

apricot and walnut loaf

serves 10–12

When selecting dried apricots or other dried fruit, look for produce that is plump and pliable, which indicates that it has been recently dried and packed. Older fruit may be leathery. Store in an airtight container at room temperature for up to 1 month or refrigerated for up to 6 months.

1½ cups (6 oz/185 g) dried apricots

1 cup (8 fl oz/250 ml) water

2 cups (10 oz/315 g) self-rising flour

½ teaspoon baking soda (bicarbonate of soda)

⅔ cup (5 oz/155 g) sugar

1 teaspoon finely shredded orange zest

¾ cup (3 oz/90 g) walnuts, finely chopped

⅓ cup (3 fl oz/90 ml) orange juice

1 egg

¼ cup (2 oz/60 g) butter, melted

❖ Preheat oven to 300°F (150°C/Gas Mark 2). Grease a 4½- x 9-inch (12- x 23-cm) loaf pan and line with parchment (baking) or waxed (greaseproof) paper.

❖ Place the dried apricots and water in a saucepan. Bring to a boil, then reduce the heat, cover, and simmer for 10 minutes, or until the apricots are tender. Drain, reserving ¼ cup (2 fl oz/60 ml) of the liquid. Cool the apricots and roughly chop.

❖ In a large mixing bowl, sift together the flour and baking soda. Stir through the sugar, orange zest, walnuts, and apricots. Make a well in the center.

❖ In a medium mixing bowl, whisk together the orange juice, egg, melted butter, and reserved apricot liquid. Add all at once to the dry ingredients and mix well.

❖ Spoon the batter into the prepared pan and bake for 50–60 minutes, or until a wooden or metal skewer inserted into the center of the cake comes out clean. Remove from oven, cool in the pan for 5 minutes, then turn out onto a wire rack to cool completely.

❖ Serve cut into slices.

nutty oatmeal pancakes

makes 8–10 pancakes
serves 4–5

Vary the flavor of this batter by experimenting with different blends of muesli or multi-grain cereals, or create your own "house" blend and make it your morning signature. Serve the pancakes with preserves (jams), fruit, or warmed maple syrup.

¾ cup (4 oz/125 g) all-purpose (plain) flour

1 teaspoon baking powder

¼ teaspoon baking soda (bicarbonate of soda)

¼ teaspoon salt

⅓ cup (1½ oz/45 g) quick-cooking rolled oats or multi-grain cereal

1 tablespoon sugar

1 egg, beaten

1 cup (8 oz/250 g) buttermilk

2 tablespoons vegetable oil

¼ cup (1 oz/30 g) chopped walnuts

◈ In a medium mixing bowl, sift together the flour, baking powder, baking soda, and salt. Stir through the rolled oats or multi-grain cereal and the sugar. Make a well in the center.

◈ In a small mixing bowl, combine the egg, buttermilk, and oil. Add egg mixture to flour mixture all at once. Stir until just blended. (The batter will be slightly lumpy.) Stir in the nuts.

◈ For each pancake, spoon about ¼ cup (2 fl oz/60 ml) of the batter onto a lightly greased preheated griddle or heavy frying pan. Cook several pancakes at a time over medium heat until their surfaces are evenly bubbled and their edges are slightly dry, 2–3 minutes. Using a spatula, turn and cook until the second side is golden brown, 2–3 minutes more. Cook the remaining batter in the same way. Serve warm.

apple and pecan cake

serves 8–10

Instead of the pecans, you could use another type of nut in this recipe, such as walnuts or lightly toasted almonds or macadamias.

2 green cooking apples, peeled

1 cup (8 oz/250 g) granulated (white) sugar

1½ cups (7 oz/220 g) all-purpose (plain) flour

1 teaspoon baking soda (bicarbonate of soda)

1 teaspoon ground cinnamon

1 teaspoon ground allspice

½ teaspoon salt

1 cup (4 oz/125 g) chopped pecans

1 egg

½ cup (4 oz/125 g) butter, melted

confectioners' (icing) sugar, for dusting

◈ Preheat oven to 375°F (190°C/Gas Mark 5). Grease an 8-inch (20-cm) square cake pan. Line the base with parchment (baking) paper.

◈ Cut the apples into large dice and mix with the sugar. In another bowl, sift together the flour, baking soda, cinnamon, allspice, and salt. Stir through the pecans.

◈ In a small mixing bowl, whisk together the egg and melted butter until combined, then add to the apple mixture. Lightly fold the sifted dry ingredients into the apple mixture, then spoon batter into the prepared pan.

◈ Bake for 45–55 minutes, or until a wooden or metal skewer inserted in the center comes out clean. Cool in the pan for 10 minutes before turning out onto a wire rack to cool completely.

◈ Sift confectioners' sugar over the top of the cake before serving.

chocolate truffle
cupcakes

makes 12

These rich little cakes
contain a double dose of
chocolate. Ice them if you
wish (see page 251) or just
decorate each cake with
a chocolate button.

½ cup (4 oz/125 g) butter

¾ cup (6 oz/185 g) sugar

2 eggs

6½ oz (200 g) bittersweet (dark) chocolate, melted

2 cups (10 oz/315 g) self-rising flour

2 tablespoons unsweetened cocoa powder

1 teaspoon baking powder

1 cup (8 fl oz/250 ml) milk

12 chocolate buttons, for decoration (optional)

◈ Preheat oven to 400°F (200°C/Gas Mark 6). Lightly grease twelve ½-cup capacity cupcake molds or line them with parchment (baking) paper cases.

◈ In a medium mixing bowl, combine the butter and sugar. With an electric mixer on medium to high speed, beat until light and fluffy. Add the eggs, one at a time, beating well after each addition. Stir in the chocolate, flour, cocoa powder, and baking powder alternately with the milk.

◈ Spoon the batter into the prepared molds and top each cake with a chocolate button, if desired. Bake for 20 minutes, or until a wooden or metal skewer inserted into the center of one of the cakes comes out clean. Cool in pan for 5 minutes, then turn out onto a wire rack to cool completely. Serve warm or cool.

enticing icings

simple chocolate icing

In a heatproof pan over a bowl of simmering water, melt 5 oz (155 g) semisweet (plain) chocolate chips and 1 tablespoon (20 g) butter or vegetable shortening. Mix to combine. Allow to cool for a few minutes before using.

cream cheese icing

In a bowl, place ½ cup (4 oz/ 125 g) softened cream cheese, 2 tablespoons softened butter, and 1½ cups (6 oz/185 g) sifted confectioner's (icing) sugar. Using an electric mixer, beat until smooth and fluffy. Swirl over tops of cakes.

date and walnut loaf

serves 10–12

Allspice is not, as its name implies, a mixture of several spices. It is the dried berry of a tree (*Pimenta dioica*) that is native to tropical America. The name does, however, describe its taste, which resembles that of a mixture of spices in which cloves predominate.

1²/₃ cups (9 oz/270 g) chopped dates

¹/₂ cup (2 oz/60 g) chopped walnuts

¹/₂ cup (4 oz/125 g) sugar

pinch salt

1 tablespoon (³/₄ oz/20 g) butter

1 teaspoon baking soda (bicarbonate of soda)

1 teaspoon ground allspice

1 cup (8 fl oz/250 ml) boiling water

1¹/₂ cups (7 oz/225 g) self-rising flour

❖ Preheat oven to 350°F (180°C/Gas Mark 4). Grease a 4- x 8-inch (10- x 20-cm) loaf pan.

❖ In a medium saucepan, combine the dates, walnuts, sugar, salt, butter, baking soda, allspice, and boiling water. Stir over low heat until the butter is melted. Set aside to cool. When cool, sift in the flour, mix well, then spoon the mixture into the prepared pan.

❖ Bake for about 45 minutes, or until a skewer inserted in the center of the cake comes out clean. Remove from oven and cool in the pan on a wire rack for 10 minutes.

❖ Turn out onto a wire rack to cool completely. Serve cut into thick slices.

food fact

If you're making a cake that calls for self-rising flour, but all you have on hand is all-purpose (plain) flour, don't worry. Self-rising flour is simply a combination of all-purpose flour and baking powder. To make your own, add 1 teaspoon baking powder to each cup of all-purpose flour. Sift together, along with any other dry ingredients, then proceed as directed in the recipe.

apricot and raisin bran loaf

makes 1 loaf

This loaf is low in fat and high in fiber, making it a healthful choice for childrens' lunchboxes or to toast for breakfast. The recipe uses soy milk rather than cows' milk, and is suitable for those who are lactose intolerant.

1 cup (6 oz/185 g) chopped dried apricots

1 cup (6½ oz/200 g) chopped raisins

1 cup (2¼ oz/70 g) All-Bran, Bran Buds, or other bran cereal

½ cup (3 oz/90 g) packed brown sugar

1½ cups (12 fl oz/375 ml) low-fat soy milk

1 cup (5 oz/150 g) self-rising flour

½ cup (3 oz/85 g) whole wheat (wholemeal) self-rising flour

1 teaspoon ground cinnamon

½ teaspoon mixed spice

butter or margarine, to serve (optional)

◈ In a medium mixing bowl, stir together the apricots, raisins, bran cereal, and brown sugar. Stir through the soy milk. Cover and set aside for at least 2 hours. The mixture may be stored overnight in the refrigerator if desired (bring it back to room temperature before proceeding with the recipe).

◈ Preheat oven to 350°F (180°C/Gas Mark 4). Grease an 8- x 4-inch (20- x 10-cm) loaf tin. Line the base with parchment (baking) paper.

◈ In a large mixing bowl, sift together the flours, cinnamon, and mixed spice. Return the husks to the bowl. Make a well in the center. Stir in the bran mixture and mix thoroughly.

◈ Spoon into the prepared pan, then use wet fingers to smooth the surface.

◈ Bake for 50–55 minutes, or until a wooden or metal skewer comes out clean when inserted into the center of the loaf. Remove from oven and cool in pan for 5 minutes before turning out onto a wire rack to cool completely. Serve, sliced, with butter or margarine, if desired.

dried fruit
tea bread

makes 2 loaves

This is a low-fat recipe in which any combination of dried fruit may be used. Make up your own mixture, or buy one pre-packaged.

2 cups (10 oz/315 g) mixed chopped dried fruit (see note)

1 cup (8 fl oz/250 ml) warm black tea, strained

1 cup (6 oz/180 g) packed brown sugar

2 tablespoons light molasses (golden syrup)

4 cups (1¼ lb/600 g) self-rising flour

1 teaspoon ground cinnamon

²/₃ cup (3 oz/85 g) chopped pecans

2 eggs, lightly beaten

❖ In a large mixing bowl, combine the dried fruit, tea, sugar, and molasses. Cover and set aside for at least 3 hours to allow the fruit to soften and plump up.

❖ Preheat oven to 315°F (160°C/Gas Mark 3). Generously grease two 8- x 4-inch (20- x-10 cm) cake pans and line bases with parchment (baking) paper.

❖ In a large mixing bowl, sift together the flour and cinnamon. Stir in the pecans. Make a well in the center.

❖ Add the eggs to the flour mixture together with the soaked fruit mixture. Stir to combine. Spoon batter into the prepared pans, then use wet fingers to smooth the surface.

❖ Bake for 50–60 minutes, or until a skewer comes out clean when inserted into the center of the loaves. Remove from oven and cool in pans for 5 minutes before turning out onto a wire rack to cool completely.

buttermilk waffles
with caramel pears

serves 4

WAFFLES

1 cup (5 oz/150 g) whole wheat
(wholemeal) self-rising flour

1 cup (5½ oz/170 g) self-rising flour

¼ cup (1¾ oz/50 g) packed brown sugar

2 eggs

⅓ cup (3 oz/90 g) butter, melted

1¾ cups (14 fl oz/440 ml) buttermilk

CARAMEL

2 oz (60 g) butter

½ cup (3 oz/90 g) packed brown sugar

1 tablespoon brandy or rum

1 cup (8 fl oz/250 ml) heavy (double) cream

2 pears, peeled, cored, and thickly sliced

◈ In a large mixing bowl, sift together the flours, returning the husks to the bowl. Stir in the brown sugar. Make a well in the center.

◈ In a medium mixing bowl, whisk together the eggs, butter, and buttermilk. Add all at once to the flour mixture. Whisk until a smooth batter forms. Add a little extra buttermilk if the batter is too thick.

◈ Heat a waffle baker and grease lightly with butter. Pour ½ cup (4 fl oz/125 ml) of the batter onto the waffle baker. Using a spatula, spread mixture to the edge of the grid. Close the lid and cook for 2–3 minutes, or until crisp.

◈ For the caramel, place the butter and sugar in a medium frying pan over low heat. Stir until the sugar has dissolved. Stir in the brandy or rum and cream. Bring to a boil and continue boiling over a low heat for 3 minutes, or until thickened slightly. Add the pear slices and cook for a further 2–3 minutes, or until the pears have softened a little.

◈ Divide the waffles into quarters, top with pears, and drizzle with the sauce.

spiced fruit loaf

makes 1 loaf

Any dried fruit, whether a
single type or a combination,
may be used for this recipe.
Try dried peaches, pears,
apples, and/or dates.

1 cup (12 oz/350 g) honey

1³/₄ oz (50 g) butter, at room temperature

1 egg, lightly beaten

2¹/₂ cups (14 oz/450 g) self-rising flour

1 teaspoon mixed spice

¹/₂ teaspoon ground nutmeg

¹/₂ teaspoon baking soda (bicarbonate of soda)

³/₄ cup (6 fl oz/185 ml) buttermilk

¹/₂ cup (2³/₄ oz/80 g) chopped blanched almonds

¹/₂ cup (4 oz/125 g) chopped prunes

¹/₂ cup (3 oz/90 g) chopped dried apricots

¹/₄ cup (1 oz/30 g) chopped raisins

✧ Preheat oven to 350°F (180°C/Gas Mark 4). Generously grease a 9- x 6-inch (23- x-15 cm) loaf tin and line base with parchment (baking) paper.

✧ In a small mixing bowl, using an electric mixer on medium to high speed, beat together the honey and butter. Add the egg and beat until creamy. Transfer to a large bowl.

✧ Sift together the flour, spice, nutmeg, and baking soda. Add alternately with the buttermilk to the butter-and-honey mixture. Stir through the almonds and dried fruit.

✧ Spoon batter into the prepared pan, then use wet fingers to smooth the surface.

✧ Bake for 45–50 minutes, or until a skewer comes out clean when inserted into the center of the loaf. Remove from oven and cool in pan for 5 minutes before turning out onto a wire rack to cool completely.

whole wheat, banana, and molasses loaf

makes 1 loaf

This loaf combines bananas, spices, and molasses to make a wholesome, warming loaf that is particularly good for winter. When freshly baked, spread the loaf with butter. When it's a day or two old, it makes excellent toast. The recipe uses a food processor for extra-quick mixing.

½ cup (4 oz/125 g) butter, chopped, at room temperature

¾ cup (4½ oz/140 g) packed brown sugar

2 eggs, lightly beaten

1 large banana, chopped

1 tablespoon light molasses (golden syrup), warmed

1 cup (5½ oz/170 g) whole wheat (wholemeal) self-rising flour

½ cup (2½ oz/75 g) self-rising flour

1 teaspoon cinnamon

½ teaspoon mixed spice

1 tablespoon light molasses (golden syrup), extra, warmed

✧ Preheat oven to 350°F (180°C/Gas Mark 4). Generously grease a 9- x 6-inch (23- x 12-cm) loaf pan and line the base with parchment (baking) paper.

✧ Place the butter and brown sugar in a food processor and process for 1–2 minutes, until pale. With the motor running, add the eggs one at a time, processing until smooth.

✧ Add the banana and light molasses and process until smooth.

✧ Sift the flours and spices together onto a sheet of parchment (baking) paper. Pour into the processor bowl all at once and process until just combined. Pour into the prepared pan.

✧ Bake until a skewer comes out clean when inserted in the center of the loaf, 35–40 minutes.

✧ Remove from oven and brush the warm cake with the extra warmed light molasses. Cool in pan for 5 minutes before turning out onto a wire rack to cool completely.

savory
quickbreads

cheese and chive
scones

makes 12 scones

1½ cups (7 oz/225 g)
self-rising flour

½ teaspoon salt

1 tablespoon (½ oz/15 g) chilled
butter, chopped

¾ cup (3 oz/90 g) finely
shredded Cheddar cheese

2 tablespoons finely
snipped chives

¾ cup (6 fl oz/180 ml) milk

extra milk, for glazing

❖ Preheat oven to 400°F (200°C/Gas Mark 6). Grease and flour a baking sheet.

❖ Sift the flour and salt into a bowl. Add the butter and, using your fingertips, rub in the butter until fine crumbs form. Add the cheese, chives, and three-fourths of the milk. Using a flat-bladed knife, mix until just combined, adding a little more milk if necessary to form a soft dough.

❖ Turn out onto a lightly floured work surface. Press out the dough until ¾ inch (2 cm) thick. Cut into rounds with a floured cutter and place on the baking sheet. Gather the scraps together, press out as before, and cut more rounds.

❖ Brush the tops with the extra milk and bake until well-colored and cooked through, about 10 minutes.

herb and yogurt
batter bread

makes 1 loaf (16 servings)

Batter breads are easier to make than ones made with a dough. Although this recipe contains yeast, there is no shaping or kneading and only one brief rise. This bread is tender, because of the addition of yogurt, and is attractively speckled with fresh herbs. It is delicious for sandwiches or to accompany soup.

2¼ cups (11 oz/340 g) all-purpose (plain) flour

1 package (7 g) active dry yeast

1 tablespoon snipped fresh basil or thyme or ¾ teaspoon crushed dried basil or thyme

½ cup (4 fl oz/125 ml) plain yogurt

½ cup (4 fl oz/125 ml) water

¼ cup (2 oz/60 g) butter or margarine

1 tablespoon sugar

½ teaspoon salt

1 egg

❖ Preheat oven to 375°F (190°C/Gas Mark 4). Grease an 8- x 4- x 2-inch (20- x 10- x 5-cm) loaf pan or a 1½-qt (1-liter) soufflé dish.

❖ In a large mixing bowl, stir together 1 cup (5 oz/150 g) of the flour, the yeast, and basil or thyme; set aside.

❖ In a medium saucepan over low heat, heat and stir the yogurt, water, butter or margarine, sugar, and salt until mixture is warm (250°–270°F/120°–130°C) and the butter or margarine is almost melted. Add to the flour mixture along with the egg. Using an electric mixer on low speed, beat for 30 seconds, scraping bowl constantly. Beat on high speed for 3 minutes. Using a wooden spoon, stir in the remaining flour. (The batter will be sticky.) Spoon batter into the prepared pan. Cover and let rise in a warm place until nearly double (about 30 minutes).

❖ Bake until golden brown and a wooden or metal skewer inserted into the center comes out clean, 35–40 minutes. If necessary, cover with foil for the last 10–15 minutes of baking to prevent overbrowning. Remove bread from pan; cool on a wire rack.

walnut bloomer bread

makes 1 loaf

This traditional English bread is normally made with yeast, but this quick version also gives splendid results. Long, plump loaves are a typically British shape. The name comes from the deep slashes on the bread's surface; when baked, these expand, or "bloom."

2 cups (11 oz/340 g) whole wheat (wholemeal) self-rising flour

2 cups (10 oz/315 g) self-rising flour, plus extra for dusting

1 teaspoon baking powder

1/2 teaspoon salt

1 1/2 cups (6 oz/185 g) roughly chopped walnuts

1 3/4 cups (14 fl oz/440 ml) milk

2 tablespoons vegetable oil

1 tablespoon light molasses (golden syrup)

◈ Preheat oven to 415°F (210°C/Gas Mark 5). Grease a baking sheet.

◈ In a large mixing bowl, sift together the flours, baking powder, and salt, returning husks to the bowl. Stir in the walnuts. Make a well in the center.

◈ In a measuring jug, combine the milk, oil, and light molasses. Add almost all the liquid to the dry ingredients. Using a flat-bladed knife, mix until just combined, adding a little more liquid if necessary to form a soft dough.

◈ Turn out onto a floured work surface and knead briefly and lightly until smooth. Shape into a loaf 10 inches (25 cm) long by 5 inches (12.5 cm) wide. Place on the prepared tray. Using a sharp knife, cut five deep, evenly spaced slashes across the top of the loaf. Sift the extra all-purpose flour over the top.

◈ Bake for 20 minutes, then reduce oven temperature to 350°F (180°C/Gas Mark 4) and cook for a further 15–20 minutes, or until the loaf is golden brown and firm and sounds hollow when tapped on the underside with your knuckles.

◈ Remove from oven, let cool in pan for 5 minutes, then transfer to a wire rack.

rye and raisin bread

makes 1 loaf

This recipe incorporates two types of flour, plus cornmeal and raisins, to make a dense, well-flavored bread.

1 cup (5½ oz/170 g) whole wheat (wholemeal) flour

1 cup (3½ oz/100 g) rye flour

1 teaspoon baking soda (bicarbonate of soda)

1¼ cups (6 oz/185 g) cornmeal

1 tablespoon sugar

⅓ cup (2 oz/60 g) chopped raisins

1½ cups (12 fl oz/375 ml) milk

½ cup (4 fl oz/125 ml) molasses (treacle)

1 teaspoon malt (brown) vinegar

❖ Preheat oven to 375°F (190°C/Gas Mark 4). Lightly grease a 9- x 5-inch (23- x 13-cm) loaf pan, line the base with parchment (baking) or greaseproof paper, then grease the paper.

❖ In a large mixing bowl, sift the flours and baking soda. Stir through the cornmeal and sugar. Add the raisins, milk, molasses, and vinegar and stir to combine.

❖ Spoon the mixture into the prepared pan and bake until a skewer inserted into the center comes out clean, about 50 minutes.

❖ Remove from oven, cool in pan for 5 minutes, then transfer to a wire rack.

recipe **hint**

Rye flour is slightly bitter, with a pleasant tang. It contains some of the gluten-forming proteins that give bread its typical structure and texture, though less than wheat flour. It may be used on its own, when it produces a dense, heavy bread, or combined with wheat flour to give a slightly lighter-textured loaf.

pumpkin bread

serves 6

Mashed pumpkin gives this bread a moist, velvety texture and a hint of sweetness. Slice it for sandwiches, or serve it with or without butter to accompany soups or salads. It is also good toasted.

1½ cups (8 oz/250 g) cooked, cooled pumpkin (see note, page 273)

1 large egg, lightly beaten

¾ cup (6 fl oz/180 ml) milk, plus extra for brushing

4 cups (1¼ lb/625 g) self-rising flour

1 teaspoon salt

3 tablespoons (1½ oz/45 g) chilled butter, chopped

1 teaspoon dried mixed herbs

all-purpose (plain) flour or cornmeal (polenta), for coating

✧ Preheat oven to 425°F (220°C/Gas 7). Grease and flour a baking sheet.

✧ In a medium bowl, mash together the pumpkin, egg, and milk until smooth.

✧ In a large mixing bowl, sift the flour and salt. Add the butter and, using your fingertips, rub in until the mixture resembles fine crumbs. Add the herbs, then stir in the pumpkin mixture. Turn out onto a floured work surface and knead lightly until a smooth dough forms.

✧ Form the dough into a mounded, round loaf and place on the prepared baking sheet. Using a sharp knife, score the top from the center outwards to make 8 wedge shapes. Brush with the extra milk, then dust with flour or cornmeal.

✧ Bake for 25 minutes, then reduce heat to 350°F (180°C/Gas Mark 4) and cook until the loaf sounds hollow when tapped on the underside with your knuckles, a further 10–15 minutes. Serve hot.

recipe hint

To yield 1½ cups cooked, mashed pumpkin, peel and seed a 1½-lb (750-g) piece of pumpkin or butternut squash. Boil, steam, or microwave until tender when pierced with a fork. Using a fork or potato masher, mash well. Let cool to lukewarm before adding other ingredients.

rye and caraway
quickbread

makes 1 loaf

The distinctive pungency of caraway seeds and the slight sourness of rye go together well. This combination is found in many of the breads of northern Europe. The addition of self-rising flour gives this recipe a lighter texture than rye flour alone.

1½ cups (7½ oz/240 g) self-rising flour

1 cup (3½ oz/100 g) rye flour

1 teaspoon baking powder

1¾ oz (50 g) chilled butter, chopped

4 teaspoons caraway seeds

1 cup (8 fl oz/250 ml) milk, plus extra for brushing

◈ Preheat oven to 415°F (210°C/Gas Mark 5). Grease a large baking sheet.

◈ In a large bowl, sift together the flours and baking powder. Add the butter and, using your fingertips, rub in until the mixture resembles fine crumbs. Stir in 3 teaspoons of the caraway seeds. Make a well in the center.

◈ Add almost all the milk to the dry ingredients. Using a flat-bladed knife, mix until just combined, adding a little more milk if necessary to form a soft dough.

◈ Turn out onto a floured work surface and knead briefly and lightly until smooth. Shape into a large round about 2 inches (5 cm) thick. Place on the prepared tray. With a sharp knife, score the top into 12 portions. Brush the top with a little extra milk and scatter over the remaining caraway seeds.

◈ Bake until golden brown and crusty and the underside of the loaf sounds hollow when tapped with your knuckles, 25–30 minutes. Cover with foil during the last 5 minutes if the crust is browning too much.

microwave herb
scone ring

serves 6-8

Scone mixtures, like others
containing quickly mixed
ingredients, are well suited
to the microwave. They may
not look as appetizing at
first as conventionally baked
scones, but when eaten
warm, slathered with butter,
they are just as delicious.

2½ cups (12 oz/375 g) self-rising flour

½ teaspoon salt, or to taste

¼ cup (2 oz/60 g) chilled butter, chopped

1–1½ cups (8–12 fl oz/250–375 ml) milk

ground black pepper to taste

2 tablespoons chopped fresh herbs, including chives
if possible

1 tablespoon (¾ oz/20 g) melted butter

✧ Grease a 20-cm (8-inch) microwave-safe ring mold.

✧ In a mixing bowl, sift together the flour and salt. Add the butter and, using your fingertips, rub in until the mixture forms fine crumbs. Add most of the milk along with the pepper and herbs. Using a flat-bladed knife, mix until just combined, adding a little more milk if necessary to form a soft dough.

✧ With floured hands, roll portions of dough into balls and arrange evenly around the ring mold, butting each piece up against the next. Glaze with melted butter.

✧ Cook on medium (50%) until the surface produces a hollow sound when tapped, 10–12 minutes.

✧ Let stand for 2–3 minutes. Serve warm with butter.

recipe hint

This recipe, and the other microwave recipes in this book, have been tested with a 700-watt microwave oven. If your oven uses a different wattage, adjust the cooking times accordingly. It is better to cook for too short a time than too long. Check often, returning the mixture to the oven for a few more minutes if it is not yet cooked.

olive and herb
damper

makes 1 loaf (8 servings)

Damper was a staple food for early European settlers in Australia. Traditionally, it is an unleavened bread made from a simple mixture of flour and water, which is cooked in the ashes of a campfire. Today the term "damper" usually refers to round, crisp-crusted, leavened loaves that resemble white bread in texture and taste. This is a savory version.

2 cups (10 oz/315 g) self-rising flour, plus extra for dusting

1 teaspoon salt

2 tablespoons (1 oz/30 g) chilled butter, chopped

1/2 cup (2 oz/60 g) grated Parmesan cheese, plus 2 tablespoons extra

1/2 cup pitted black olives, sliced

1 tablespoon chopped fresh rosemary

1/2 cup (4 fl oz/125 ml) milk, plus extra for brushing

1/4 cup (2 fl oz/60 ml) water

◈ Preheat oven to 415°C (210°C/Gas Mark 5). Grease a baking sheet and dust lightly with the extra flour.

◈ In a large mixing bowl, sift the flour and salt. Add the butter and, using your fingertips, rub in until mixture resembles fine crumbs.

◈ Stir in the Parmesan, olives, and rosemary. In a small measuring jug, combine the milk and water and add most of the liquid to the flour mixture. Using a flat-bladed knife, mix until just combined, adding a little more liquid if necessary to form a soft dough.

◈ Turn out onto a lightly floured work surface and knead briefly and lightly until smooth. Shape dough into a ball, then place on prepared baking sheet and press out into a round about ¾ inch (2 cm) thick. Using a sharp knife, score dough deeply into 8 wedges. Brush with a little of the extra milk and sprinkle with the extra cheese.

◈ Bake until golden brown and crusty, about 25 minutes.

popovers

makes 6

Crisp, puffy popovers are a real crowd-pleaser. Serve them as an appetizer or with the main meal. As soon as you remove them from the oven, gently prick their surfaces to let the steam escape.

1 tablespoon shortening, for greasing

2 eggs, beaten

1 cup (8 fl oz/250 ml) milk

1 tablespoon vegetable oil

1 cup (5 oz/150 g) all-purpose (plain) flour

1/4 teaspoon salt

◈ Preheat oven to 400°F (200°C/Gas Mark 5). Using ½ teaspoon shortening for each cup, grease the bottom and sides of six 6-fl oz (185-ml) custard cups (ramekins) or the cups of a popover pan. If using custard cups, place them in a large baking pan; set aside.

◈ In a medium mixing bowl, combine the eggs, milk, and oil. Using a wire whisk or rotary beater, beat until combined. Add the flour and salt. Beat until mixture is smooth. Spoon into the prepared cups, filling them half full. Bake until very firm, about 40 minutes.

◈ Immediately after removing them from the oven, prick each popover with a fork to let steam escape. Then, if crisper popovers are desired, return them to the oven for 5–10 minutes more, or until of the desired crispness. (Be sure the oven is turned off.) Serve hot.

food fact

Popovers are similar to Yorkshire puddings, traditional British batter puddings that are cooked in the sizzling drippings from roast beef, then served to accompany it.

herb-filled
scone foldovers

makes about 12

A simple scone mixture
gets a savory update with
the addition of herbs and
buttermilk. Serve these
foldovers warm with butter
or cream cheese, if desired.

HERB FILLING

¼ cup (1 oz/30 g) grated Parmesan cheese

1 tablespoon butter, at room temperature

1 tablespoon finely chopped parsley

1 tablespoon finely shredded basil

1 tablespoon finely chopped oregano leaves

SCONE DOUGH

2 cups (10 oz/315 g) self-rising flour

1 oz (30 g) chilled butter, chopped

1 cup (8 fl oz/250 ml) buttermilk, plus extra for brushing

◈ Preheat oven to 415°F (210°C/Gas Mark 5). Grease a large baking sheet.

◈ For the herb filling, in a small bowl, combine the Parmesan, butter, parsley, basil, and oregano. Stir and set aside.

◈ For the scone dough, in a large bowl, sift the flour. Add the chopped butter and, using your fingertips, rub in until the mixture forms coarse crumbs. Make a well in the center.

◈ Add almost all the buttermilk to the dry ingredients. Using a flat-bladed knife, mix until just combined, adding a little more buttermilk if necessary to form a soft dough.

◈ Turn out onto a floured work surface and knead briefly and lightly until smooth. Pat or roll the dough out to ¼-inch (5-mm) thickness. Using a 2¾-inch (7-cm) cutter, cut out rounds. Brush edges of rounds with the extra buttermilk. Lightly press a half teaspoon of the filling into the center of each round. Fold the round in half and pinch the edges firmly to seal.

◈ Place rounds on the prepared tray, spacing them well apart so that they have room to expand. Lightly brush tops with extra buttermilk.

◈ Bake until well risen and golden brown, about 12 minutes.

whole wheat herb
damper

makes 1 loaf

Although dampers are traditionally plain, modern interpretations, such as this recipe, may be flavored. Like most dampers, it is best served warm, spread with fresh butter if desired.

3 cups (1 lb/500 g) whole wheat (wholemeal) self-rising flour

1 cup (5 oz/150 g) self-rising flour

1 teaspoon baking powder

1/2 teaspoon salt

1 cup (2 oz/60 g) chopped mixed fresh herbs (such as parsley, chives, thyme, and rosemary, or 3–4 herbs of your choice)

2 cups (16 fl oz/500 ml) milk

2 tablespoons vegetable oil

1 tablespoon light molasses (golden syrup)

1/2 cup (1 1/2 oz/45 g) wheatgerm, for kneading

✦ Preheat oven to 415°F (210°C/Gas Mark 5). Grease a large baking sheet.

✦ In a large bowl, sift together the flours, baking powder, and salt, returning the husks to the bowl. Stir in the herbs. Make a well in the center.

✦ In a pitcher, combine the milk, oil, and light molasses. Add almost all of the liquid to the dry ingredients. Using a flat-bladed knife, mix until just combined, adding a little more liquid if necessary to form a soft dough.

✦ Turn out onto a work surface that has been sprinkled with the wheatgerm. Knead the dough briefly and lightly until smooth.

✦ Place on the prepared tray and pat into a 10-inch (25-cm) round. Brush with a little extra milk and sprinkle with a little of the wheatgerm. With a sharp knife, cut a cross in the top.

✦ Bake for 20 minutes, then reduce oven temperature to 350°F (180°C/Gas Mark 4) and cook until golden brown and firm and the loaf sounds hollow when the underside is tapped with your knuckles, 20 minutes more.

beer breads
with parmesan
and rosemary

makes 2 loaves

Beer gives bread the
delicious taste of yeast,
without the lengthy rising
time. This loaf is studded
with rosemary, producing a
wonderful flavor and aroma.

3¼ cups (11 oz/340 g) self-rising flour

½ teaspoon baking powder

½ teaspoon salt

1¾ oz (50 g) chilled butter, chopped

1 tablespoon sugar

½ cup (2 oz/60 g) grated Parmesan cheese

1 tablespoon chopped fresh rosemary

1½ cups (12 fl oz/375 ml) beer

all-purpose (plain) flour, for sprinkling

10 small sprigs rosemary

❖ Preheat oven to 415°F (210°C/Gas Mark 5). Grease a large baking sheet.

❖ In a large bowl, sift together the flour, baking powder, and salt. Add the butter and, using your fingertips, rub in until the mixture resembles coarse crumbs. Stir in the sugar, Parmesan, and rosemary. Make a well in the center.

❖ Add almost all the beer to the dry ingredients. Using a flat-bladed knife, mix until just combined, adding a little more beer if necessary to form a soft dough.

❖ Turn out onto a floured work surface and knead briefly and lightly until smooth. Divide the dough in half. Knead each half into 2 even-sized balls. Place on the prepared tray, spacing them well apart so that they have room to expand. Sprinkle with a little extra flour. Using scissors, snip the surface of the loaves all over at 2-inch (5-cm) intervals. Evenly nestle the rosemary sprigs into the cuts in the surface of the loaf.

❖ Bake until golden brown and firm and the loaf sounds hollow when the underside is tapped with your knuckles, 20–25 minutes.

chunky corn bread

serves 6

Although corn was a native American crop, early colonists were the first to make bread from the ground meal. Wholesome, savory-sweet corn bread is a staple in diners across the United States, but particularly in the South and Southwest, where corn remains a staple crop.

1 cup (5 oz/150 g) all-purpose (plain) flour

1 teaspoon salt

1 tablespoon baking powder

1 cup (5 oz/150 g) yellow cornmeal

1 cup (8 fl oz/250 ml) milk

2 tablespoons honey

2 eggs, well beaten

1/3 cup (3 oz/90 g) unsalted butter, melted and cooled

1/2 cup (3 1/2 oz/100 g) corn kernels (fresh, drained canned, or thawed frozen)

◈ Preheat oven to 400°F (200°C/Gas Mark 5). Grease an 8-inch (20-cm) square baking pan.

◈ In a large bowl, sift together the flour, salt, and baking powder. Stir through the cornmeal.

◈ In a large measuring cup, whisk together the milk, honey, and eggs.

◈ Using a wooden spoon, stir the egg mixture into the cornmeal mixture until well combined. Stir in the melted butter, then gently mix in the corn kernels. Pour the batter into the prepared pan.

◈ Bake until the center is firm to the touch, 18–20 minutes. Cut into squares and serve hot.

recipe variations

Cornbread is traditionally made in a cast-iron frying pan. If you like, add a cup of chopped pork cracklings for crunch, or stir in a dash of maple syrup to sweeten. You could also try adding ½ teaspoon crushed dried thyme or 2 oz (60 g) of any shredded mild melting cheese or Cheddar cheese.

pissaladière

serves 6–8

TOPPING

¼ cup (2 fl oz/60 ml) olive oil

3 onions, thinly sliced

2 cloves garlic

1 tablespoon fresh thyme leaves

1 tablespoon tomato paste

SCONE DOUGH

1 cup (150 g/5 oz) all-purpose (plain) flour

1 cup (150 g/5 oz) self-rising flour

1¾ oz (50 g) chilled butter, chopped

¾ cup (6 fl oz/185 ml) milk

TO FINISH

1 oz (30 g) can anchovy fillets, drained, sliced in half lengthways

16 pitted black olives

extra olive oil, for drizzling

For the topping, in a large saucepan over low heat, warm the oil. Add the onions, garlic, and thyme leaves. Cook, covered, stirring frequently, until the onion is very soft and lightly golden, about 40 minutes. Stir in the tomato paste. Set aside to cool.

Preheat oven to 425°F (220°C/Gas Mark 5). Grease a 12-inch (30-cm) pizza tray.

For the scone dough, in a large bowl, sift together the flours. Add the butter and, using your fingertips, rub in until the mixture forms coarse crumbs. Make a well in the center.

Add almost all the milk to the dry ingredients. Using a flat-bladed knife, mix until just combined, adding a little more milk if necessary to form a soft dough.

Turn out onto a floured work surface and knead briefly and lightly until smooth. Roll to fit the pizza tray evenly, pushing the edges of the dough up a little to make a rim.

Spread evenly with the onion mixture, leaving the rim uncovered.

To finish, arrange the anchovy fillets over the top in a lattice pattern and place an olive in the center of each diamond. Drizzle over a little of the extra oil.

Bake until the dough is brown and crisp, 20–25 minutes. Serve hot.

makes 1 loaf

FILLING

*3 slices prosciutto,
finely chopped*

*½ cup (2 oz/60 g) finely
shredded Cheddar cheese*

*¼ cup (½ oz/15 g)
chopped chives*

*¼ cup (½ oz/15 g) chopped
flat-leaf (Italian) parsley*

*1 tablespoon fresh
thyme leaves*

SCONE DOUGH

*2½ cups (12 oz/375 g)
self-rising flour*

1 teaspoon baking powder

*1¾ oz (50 g) chilled butter,
chopped*

*⅓ cup (1¼ oz/35 g) grated
Parmesan cheese*

1 cup (8 fl oz/250 ml) milk

extra milk, for brushing

❖ Preheat oven to 415°F (210°C/Gas Mark 5).
Grease a baking sheet.

❖ For filling, in a small bowl, combine prosciutto,
Cheddar, chives, parsley, and thyme. Set aside.

❖ For scone dough, in a large bowl, sift together
flour and baking powder. Using fingertips, rub in
butter. Stir in Parmesan. Make a well in the center.

❖ Add most of the milk to the dry ingredients.
Using a flat-bladed knife, mix until a soft dough
forms, adding a little more milk if necessary.

❖ Turn out onto a floured work surface and knead
briefly and lightly until smooth. Divide the dough
into three equal portions. Pat or roll each portion
into an 8-inch (20-cm) round.

❖ Place one round onto prepared baking sheet.
Sprinkle with half the filling. Place another round
on top and sprinkle with remaining filling. Place
the last round on top. Pinch edges together to seal.

❖ Using a sharp knife, score the top into 8 even
wedges. Brush the top with the extra milk.

❖ Bake for 15 minutes, then reduce oven to 350°F
(180°C/Gas Mark 4) and cook 10–15 minutes more,
or until well risen and golden brown. Serve warm.

herb and prosciutto
scone loaf

buttermilk corn bread

serves 4–6

2 cups (10 oz/315 g)
yellow cornmeal (polenta)

½ cup (2½ oz/75 g) all-purpose (plain) flour

½ teaspoon baking powder

1 teaspoon salt

1¾ cups (14 fl oz/440 ml) buttermilk

1 large egg, lightly beaten

⅓ cup (3 fl oz/90 ml) butter or
bacon drippings

melted butter, extra

❖ Preheat oven to 425°F (220°C/Gas Mark 6).

❖ In a large bowl, combine the cornmeal, flour, baking powder, and salt. Add the buttermilk, egg, and half the butter or drippings. Mix well.

❖ Heat the remaining butter or drippings in a large cast-iron frying pan or 8-inch (20-cm) square cake pan. Pour in batter, place in oven, and bake for 10 minutes. Brush surface with the extra melted butter and bake for a further 10 minutes, or until golden brown. Serve warm, cut into squares.

tomato pesto crescents

makes 12

FILLING

½ cup (¾ oz/25 g) grated Parmesan cheese

¼ cup (½ oz/15 g) finely shredded basil leaves

4 drained, oil-packed,
sun-dried or semi-dried tomatoes,
finely chopped

SCONE DOUGH

2 cups (10 oz/315 g)
self-rising flour

2 tablespoons (1 oz/30 g)
chilled butter, cubed

¾ cup (6 fl oz/185 ml) milk

¼ cup (2 fl oz/60 ml)
bought pesto sauce

❖ Preheat oven to 415°F (210°C/Gas Mark 5). Grease a large baking sheet.

❖ For the filling, in a small bowl combine the Parmesan cheese, basil, and tomatoes.

❖ For the scone dough, sift the flour into a large bowl. Using fingertips, rub in the butter. Make a well in the center.

❖ Add most of the milk to the flour mixture. Using a flat-bladed knife, mix until a soft dough forms, adding a little more milk if necessary.

❖ Turn out onto a floured surface and knead briefly and lightly until smooth. Pat or roll the dough out to a 12-inch (30-cm) round.

❖ Spread the pesto evenly over the dough, then sprinkle with the filling mixture. Using a sharp knife, cut dough into 12 even wedges. Roll each wedge from the wide end to the pointed end. Seal ends with a little milk. Place pieces, sealed ends up, onto the baking sheet and form each into a crescent shape. Bake until golden brown, about 15 minutes. Serve hot.

irish soda bread

makes 1 loaf

2 cups (11 oz/340 g) whole wheat (wholemeal) flour

2 cups (10 oz/315 g) all-purpose (plain) flour, plus extra for sprinkling

1 teaspoon baking soda (bicarbonate of soda)

1 teaspoon salt

2 tablespoons (1 oz/30 g) butter, melted

2 cups (16 fl oz/ 500 ml) buttermilk

❖ Preheat oven to 400°F (200°C/Gas Mark 5). Grease a baking sheet.

❖ In a large mixing bowl, sift together the flours, baking soda, and salt, returning the husks to the bowl. Make a well in the center.

❖ Add the melted butter and most of the buttermilk to the flour mixture. Using a flat-bladed knife, mix until just combined, adding a little more buttermilk if necessary to form a soft dough.

❖ Turn out onto a floured surface and knead for 3 minutes until smooth and elastic. Shape into an 8-inch (20-cm) round and flatten to about 2 inches (5 cm) thick. Place on prepared tray. Brush top with remaining buttermilk and sprinkle generously with extra flour. Using a sharp knife, make 2 parallel slashes 1 inch (2.5 cm) deep across the top.

❖ Bake for 35–40 minutes, or until golden brown and crusty. Cover with foil during the last 5 minutes if the crust is browning too much. Test for doneness by tapping base with knuckles. When cooked, the bread will sound hollow.

❖ Transfer to a wire rack, cover with a clean tea towel, and leave to cool.

ratatouille mini pizzas

makes about 24

*2 cups (10 oz/315 g)
self-rising flour*

*2 tablespoons (1 oz/30 g)
chilled butter, cubed*

*½ cup (2 oz/60 g)
grated Parmesan cheese*

*1 tablespoon
fresh thyme leaves*

¾ cup (6 fl oz/185 ml) milk

*8 oz (250 g) bought mixed
char-grilled vegetables, such
as eggplant (aubergine),
zucchini (courgette),
artichokes, or red bell
pepper (capsicum)*

*⅓ cup (3 fl oz/90 ml) bought
tomato pasta sauce*

❖ Preheat oven to 415°F (210°C/Gas Mark 5). Butter two large baking sheets.

❖ In a large bowl, sift the flour. Add the chopped butter and, using your fingertips, rub in until the mixture resembles coarse crumbs. Stir in the Parmesan and thyme. Make a well in the center.

❖ Add most of the milk to the flour mixture. Using a flat-bladed knife, mix until just combined, adding a little extra milk if needed to form a soft dough.

❖ Turn out onto a floured surface and knead briefly and lightly until smooth. Pat or roll the dough out to a ¼-inch (5-mm) thickness. Using a 2½-inch (6-cm) cutter, cut into rounds. Place rounds on the prepared tray. Gather together the scraps, re-roll, and cut out more rounds.

❖ Slice or cut the vegetables into small pieces. Spread the pasta sauce thinly over the rounds and top each with 3 pieces of the vegetables.

❖ Bake until golden brown, 10–12 minutes. Serve hot.

potato and olive
mini scones

makes about 14 mini scones

These mini scones make excellent appetizers to serve with drinks. Make a double batch — you'll find that they're very popular.

8 oz (250 g) potatoes, peeled and cubed

¾ cup (6 fl oz/185 ml) light (single) cream, plus extra for brushing

2 cups (10 oz/315 g) self-rising flour

½ teaspoon salt

1 oz (30 g) chilled butter, cubed

⅓ cup (2 oz/60 g) finely chopped black olives

⅓ cup (¾ oz/20 g) chopped parsley

❧ Steam or microwave the potatoes until cooked; drain and mash. Gradually whisk in the light cream. Set aside to cool.

❧ Preheat oven to 415°F (210°C/Gas Mark 5). Grease a large baking sheet.

❧ In a large bowl, sift together the flour and salt. Add the butter and, using your fingertips, rub in until the mixture resembles coarse crumbs. Stir in the olives and parsley. Make a well in the center.

❧ Add the potato and cream mixture to the dry ingredients. Using a flat-bladed knife, mix until just combined, adding a little extra cream or water if necessary to form a soft dough.

❧ Turn out onto a floured work surface and knead briefly and lightly until smooth. Pat or roll the dough out to a ¾-inch (2-cm) thickness. Using a floured 2-inch (5-cm) cutter, cut into rounds. Place close together on the prepared tray. Gather together the scraps, re-roll, and cut more rounds. Brush lightly with the extra cream.

❧ Bake until well risen and golden brown, 12–15 minutes.

pumpkin and pecan cob

makes 1 loaf

"Cob" is a British term given
to a round, mounded loaf
of bread, sometimes with
a knob on top, as in this
savory-sweet recipe.

10 oz (315 g) pumpkin, peeled, seeded, and cubed

2 cups (10 oz/315 g) self-rising flour

1 teaspoon baking powder

1 teaspoon ground nutmeg

2 tablespoons (1 oz/30 g) chilled butter, chopped

3/4 cup (3 oz/90 g) chopped pecans

1/2 cup (4 fl oz/125 ml) milk, plus extra for brushing

2 tablespoons pumpkin seeds

✧ Steam or microwave the pumpkin until cooked; drain and mash. Set aside to cool.

✧ Preheat oven to 415°F (210°C/Gas Mark 5). Grease a baking sheet.

✧ In a large bowl, sift together the flour, baking powder, and nutmeg. Add the butter and, using fingertips, rub in until the mixture resembles coarse crumbs. Stir in the chopped pecans. Make a well in the center.

✧ Add the cooled pumpkin and almost all the milk to the dry ingredients. Using a flat-bladed knife, mix until just combined, adding a little extra milk if necessary to form a soft dough. Turn out onto a floured work surface and knead briefly and lightly until smooth.

✧ Pull away ⅙th of the dough. Knead both pieces of the dough and form each into a ball. Place the larger ball on the prepared tray and, using two fingers, make a deep indentation in the center. Brush with extra milk.

✧ Elongate the small ball of dough to fit into the indentation in the larger round. Brush knob with milk and scatter the seeds all over the top of the cob.

✧ Bake for 15 minutes, then reduce temperature to 350°F (180°C/Gas Mark 4) and bake until golden brown and the underside of the loaf sounds hollow when tapped with your knuckles, 15–20 minutes more. Cool in pan for 5 minutes, then transfer to a wire rack.

oatmeal finger bread

makes 1 loaf

This bread takes its name from the rectangles into which is is cut. Try it dipped in winter soups, or topped with cream cheese, lox (smoked salmon), capers, and thinly sliced red (Spanish) onions.

2 cups (11 oz/340 g) whole wheat (wholemeal) self-rising flour

1 cup (5 oz/150 g) self-rising flour

1 teaspoon salt

1 teaspoon baking powder

1¾ oz (50 g) chilled butter, chopped

1 cup (3½ oz/100 g) medium quick-cooking rolled oats, plus extra for sprinkling

1 tablespoon light molasses (golden syrup), warmed

1½ cups (12 fl oz/375 ml) milk, plus extra for brushing

❖ Preheat oven to 415°F (210°C/Gas Mark 5). Grease a baking sheet.

❖ In a large bowl, sift together the flours, salt, and baking powder, returning the husks to the bowl. Add the butter and, using fingertips, rub in until the mixture resembles coarse crumbs. Stir through the rolled oats. Make a well in the center.

❖ Add the light molasses and almost all the milk to the dry ingredients. Using a flat-bladed knife, mix until just combined, adding a little more milk if necessary to form a soft dough.

❖ Turn out onto a floured work surface and knead briefly and lightly until smooth.

❖ Divide dough into 6 even-sized pieces. Shape each piece into a rectangle. Arrange them in a row, just touching, on the prepared tray. Brush with extra milk and sprinkle with extra oats.

❖ Bake for 15 minutes, then reduce oven temperature to 350°F (180°C/Gas Mark 4) and bake until golden brown and the fingers sound hollow when the underside is tapped with your knuckles, a further 15–20 minutes.

onion and poppy seed
quickbread

makes 1 loaf (10–12 servings)

Poppy seeds add delicate crunch and subtle earthiness, and they team particularly well with onions. There are two types; unless white poppy seeds are specified, assume that the commoner black (or blue) are meant. Both types come from the opium poppy, but by the time the seeds have formed, the plant's narcotic effect is gone.

¼ cup (2 fl oz/60 ml) olive oil

2 onions, thinly sliced

3 cups (14 oz/450 g) self-rising flour

1¼ oz (35 g) sachet dried French onion soup mix

1 cup (8 fl oz/250 ml) milk

½ cup (4 fl oz/125 ml) plain yogurt

2 teaspoons poppy seeds

✧ in a large frying pan over low heat, warm the oil. When hot, add the onions and cook for 20 minutes, stirring frequently, until lightly golden. Set aside to cool.

✧ Preheat oven to 400°F (200°C/Gas Mark 5). Grease a large baking sheet.

✧ In a large mixing bowl, sift the flour. Stir in the onion soup mix. Make a well in the center.

✧ In a jug, combine the milk and yogurt. Add almost all the liquid to the dry ingredients, together with half the cooked onion slices. Using a flat-bladed knife, mix until just combined, adding a little more of the liquid if needed to form a soft dough.

✧ Turn out onto a floured work surface and knead briefly and lightly until smooth.

✧ Place on the prepared tray and form into a 10-inch (25-cm) long elongated loaf. Spoon over the remaining onions and sprinkle with poppy seeds.

✧ Bake for 20 minutes, then reduce oven temperature to 350°F (180°C/Gas Mark 4) and cook until golden brown and firm and the loaf sounds hollow when the underside is tapped with your knuckles, 15 minutes more. Cover with foil during the last 5 minutes if the onion is browning too much. Cool on baking sheet for 5 minutes, then transfer to a wire rack.

glossary

apples

Apples add moisture and sweetness to muffins and quickbreads. Suitable varieties for baking include Jonathan, Granny Smith, and Golden Delicious. Choose unblemished, firm fruit; store in the refrigerator crisper.

berries

Berries of all types are favorite additions to muffins and tea breads. Select unbruised berries with a vibrant color and an inviting fragrance. Store them, unwashed and loosely covered, in a single layer on a tray lined with paper towels in the refrigerator for several days.

candied fruit and peel

Candying fruits such as cherries, pineapple, citron, or strips of citrus peel in sugar syrup sweetens and preserves them. They add flavor and chewiness to baked goods.

citrus peel

Aromatic oils stored in the thin colored skin, or zest, of oranges and lemons infuse baked goods with a tart-sweet flavor and a delicate perfume. Use only the topmost layer of skin, never the bitter white pith beneath. Select firm, heavy citrus fruit with good color; refrigerate for up to 3 weeks.

coconut

Shredded (desiccated) or flaked, sweetened or unsweetened, dried coconut is often used in muffins and quickbreads. It keeps for months in an airtight container.

cooking fats

Butter, margarine, vegetable shortening, and vegetable oils enrich and tenderize breads and help develop golden crusts. Butter and margarine are interchangeable in almost any muffin or quickbread recipe;

use only regular stick margarine, not diet, whipped, or liquid forms. Shortening is a vegetable oil–based fat that stays solid at room temperature. Vegetable oil is often used in quickbreads. Butter and margarine will keep for 1 month in the refrigerator, or for up to 6 months in the freezer. Store shortening at room temperature for up to 1 year. Store oils in a cool, dark place.

crystallized (glacé) ginger

Sugar-coated candied pieces of the rhizome of a semitropical plant, crystallized (candied or glacé) ginger punctuates baked goods with an intriguing hot-sweetness. Store in an airtight container for up to 6 months.

dairy products

Milk, cream, and other dairy foods are basic ingredients in most breads. They moisten the dough or batter, add richness, refine the crumb, and help color the crust. Acidic products such as buttermilk, yogurt, and sour cream add a tangy flavor; in quick breads that use baking soda, they also help activate leavening. Chill all dairy products.

dried fruit

When fruits such as grapes, cranberries, apricots, or cherries are dried, the natural flavor intensifies and the sweetness becomes concentrated. Dried fruit is a classic ingredient for breads and muffins. Unopened packages of dried fruit will stay wholesome almost indefinitely. Once opened, refrigerate in a plastic container.

dried tomatoes

Dehydrated tomatoes are chewy, with an intense flavor. Once opened, store oil-packed dried tomatoes in an airtight container in the refrigerator for several months. Store dry-packed tomatoes in an airtight container at room temperature for 6 months to 1 year.

eggs

Quickbreads and muffins depend on eggs for flavor, tenderness, richness, and color. The shell color—brown or white—is purely superficial; there is no difference in quality or taste. Refrigerate eggs in the carton for up to 5 weeks.

flours

Wheat flour is the main structure-building ingredient in muffins and quickbreads. All-purpose (plain) flour has a medium protein content that makes it suitable for most baking uses. Self-rising flour is simply all-purpose flour with baking powder added (the ratio is 1 teaspoon baking powder per 1 cup/5 oz/155 g flour). Whole wheat (wholemeal) flour is coarsely milled from the entire wheat kernel. Store all-purpose and self-rising flours in an airtight container for 10–15 months; store whole wheat flour for up to 5 months. Alternatively, freeze or refrigerate for longer storage.

graham crackers

These flat savory cookies (wholemeal biscuits) are made with a coarsely ground whole wheat (wholemeal) flour, and are named after nineteenth-century American nutritionist Sylvester Graham. In baking, graham cracker crumbs add texture and a subtle sweetness to batters and crusts. Once opened, rewrap the package tightly and store in a cool spot.

herbs

Savory muffins and breads often use highly flavored herbs such as rosemary, parsley, basil, and sage. To store fresh herbs, wrap in paper towels in a plastic bag and refrigerate. Dried herbs are found with other seasonings in all supermarkets. Store them away from light, heat, and moisture for 6 months to 2 years.

nuts

Because of their richness, texture, and flavor, pine nuts, walnuts, hazelnuts, almonds, and cashews are used often in muffin and quickbread batters and fillings. Packaged or in bulk, a good selection of these and many other nuts is available at any supermarket. Refrigerate or freeze them, tightly covered, to keep them fresh.

olives

Olives are either cured for eating or pressed for their oil, and breads use both forms. Underripe olives are green, with a salty, tart flavor; as they ripen, they darken to an inky black and develop a mellow and smooth taste. They are available in cans, jars, or in bulk, and may be plain or marinated.

seeds

As a bread or muffin topping or mixed into the dough, crunchy aniseed, caraway, poppy, and sesame seeds concentrate a wallop of flavor in each tiny, crunchy morsel. Aniseed tastes faintly of licorice; crescent-shaped caraway is smoky sweet; slate-blue poppy is slightly sweet and nutlike; sesame, both white and black, has an earthy nuttiness. Seeds are sold in the spice section of supermarkets or at specialty stores. Poppy and sesame seeds contain oils that can turn rancid; store them in the refrigerator or freezer.

sugars

Sugar plays an important role in bread and muffin making—as a food for yeast, a sweetener, a browning agent for crusts, and a tenderizer for crumb. Granulated (white) sugar is the type most commonly used in baking. When more finely ground, it becomes superfine (caster) sugar. For most recipes, granulated and superfine sugars are interchangeable. Brown sugar is a mixture of granulated sugar and molasses that adds a rich, deep flavor; dark brown sugar has extra molasses. Confectioners' (icing) sugar is powdered and mixed with a little cornstarch to prevent caking. Store sugars indefinitely in airtight containers.

sweeteners, liquid

Some recipes in this book call for a liquid, rather than a solid form of sugar. Made by bees from floral nectar, honey is sweet and sticky and imparts rich flavor and perfume to batters, doughs, and fillings. Molasses, both the mildly sweet light (golden syrup) and the full-bodied dark (treacle), is a by-product of sugar-cane refining. Corn syrup is a form of sugar refined from corn; light corn syrup is slightly sweet and bland, while dark corn syrup tastes like molasses. Unopened bottles of syrup will last up to a year in a cool spot; after opening, store as directed on the label. Syrup and honey will pour off more freely from a measuring spoon or cup if either is first lightly oiled.

index

Page numbers in italics refer to photographs.

a note on measurements

U.S. cup measurements are used throughout this book. Slight adjustments may need to be made to quantities if Imperial or metric measures are used.

acknowledgments

Weldon Owen wishes to thank the following people for their help in producing this book: Nancy Sibtain (indexing); Angela Handley (proofreading).

loaf butters...
walnut dam...
lemon corn...
chocolate b...
teacake coo...
gingerbread...